The Precious Gem of Hidden Literature

The Precious Gem of Hidden Literature:
Francis Bacon 1576-1655
Ryan Murtha

RESOURCE *Publications* • Eugene, Oregon

THE PRECIOUS GEM OF HIDDEN LITERATURE
Francis Bacon 1576–1655

Copyright © 2022 Ryan Murtha. All rights reserved. Except for brief quotations in critical publications or reviews, no part of this book may be reproduced in any manner without prior written permission from the publisher. Write: Permissions, Wipf and Stock Publishers, 199 W. 8th Ave., Suite 3, Eugene, OR 97401.

Resource Publications
An Imprint of Wipf and Stock Publishers
199 W. 8th Ave., Suite 3
Eugene, OR 97401

www.wipfandstock.com

PAPERBACK ISBN: 978-1-6667-3840-7
HARDCOVER ISBN: 978-1-6667-9905-7
EBOOK ISBN: 978-1-6667-9906-4

We do not know half enough about Lord Bacon—the first realist in all the highest sense of the word—to know everything he did, everything he willed, and everything he experienced in his inmost soul . . . Let the critics go to hell!

Friedrich Nietzsche, *Ecce Homo*

Invest me in my motley; give me leave
To speak my mind, and I will through and through
Cleanse the foul body of the infected world,
If they will patiently receive my medicine.

As You Like It

Contents

Introduction	xiii
1. *Anti-Machiavel*	1
Parallelisms	10
2. *The Anatomie of the Minde*	39
Parallelisms	44
3. *The French Academy*	62
Parallelisms	64
4. *Vindiciae contra tyrannos*	89
Parallelisms	92
5. *Don Quixote*	106
Parallelisms	114
6. The Alchemy of Eugenius Philalethes	122
Appendix: *The Labyrinth of the World and the Paradise of the Heart* (1631)	133

History of the Royal Society (1667) with Bacon as *Artium Instaurator*, "restorer of the arts"

Introduction

Contemporaries of Sir Francis Bacon (1561-1626) eulogized him as "a muse more choice than the nine muses" who "showered the age with frequent volumes" and "filled the world with works"; "the very nerve of genius, the marrow of persuasion, the golden stream of eloquence, the precious gem of hidden literature."[1] Ben Jonson's *Timber*, published posthumously in 1641, states that Bacon "performed that in our tongue which may be compared, or preferred, either to insolent Greece or haughty Rome . . . he may be named and stand as the mark and acme of our language." This is somewhat puzzling, as Bacon published just three books in English during his life, the *Essays* (in successively expanded editions, 1597, 1612, 1625), *The Advancement of Learning* (1605), and *The History of the Reign of King Henry VII* (1622). Even more strangely, Jonson (who was sparing in his praise of other writers) had already bestowed the same encomium upon Shakespeare in the 1623 First Folio:

> Leave thee alone for the comparison
> Of all that insolent Greece or haughty Rome
> Sent forth, or since did from their ashes come.

An early claim that Bacon wrote anonymously occurred in 1599.[2] After English authorities published an account of a plot to poison Queen Elizabeth's saddle, an anonymous writer ascribed the state's "smooth penned pamphlet" to "*M. Smokey-swynes flesh*, at the instance of Sir R.C." (i.e., Francis Bacon writing at the behest of Secretary of State Robert Cecil). This is again rather strange, as Bacon had only published a small book of ten essays and some religious meditations in his own name, very little to inform attribution of other tracts. Thomas Tenison, who crowned two monarchs as Archbishop of Canterbury, edited a volume of Bacon's previously unpublished materials in 1679, in which he wrote "those who have true skill in the works of the Lord Verulam, like great masters in painting, can tell by the design, the strength, the way of colouring, whether he was the author of this or the other piece, though

---

[1] Rawley, William. *Memoriæ honoratissimi domini Francisci, Baronis de Verulamio, Vice-Comitis Sancti Albani sacrum.* London: John Haviland, 1626. (Translated from Latin)
[2] Stewart, Alan. "Rethinking Authorship Through Collaboration" in *Renaissance Transformations: The Making of Writing in Renaissance England.* Eds. Margaret Healy and Thomas Healy. Edinburgh: Edinburgh University Press, 2009.

his name be not to it."³ According to Brian Vickers, editor of the Oxford *Major Works*, Bacon had a substantial body of anonymous work and was reluctant to have his name in print:

> although Bacon had a wide and diverse literary output by 1597 (enough to fill several hundred pages of Spedding's edition of his *Occasional Works*), none of it had been publicly acknowledged as his composition. Indeed, it was only due to an impending plagiarization that his name finally appeared in print that year, to forestall the unauthorized publication of his *Essays* . . . Had Serger not attempted his unauthorized edition, Bacon's first appearance in print might have been as the author of *The Advancement of Learning* (1605), that bold attempt to persuade King James to initiate a total reformation of study and research in his new kingdom.⁴

It is not known when Bacon began writing; the present study explores a hypothesis advanced by William Smedley, who edited the journal of the Francis Bacon Society from 1910-17. Smedley undertook the task of reconstituting Bacon's personal library, eventually assembling several hundred books annotated in Bacon's handwriting, many of which were acquired by the Folger Shakespeare Library. One of the volumes held at the Folger is a copy of *The Anatomie of the Minde* with corrections in Bacon's hand; it was published in 1576, the year Bacon left Cambridge. Smedley believed this was Bacon's first book, composed at school (the *Anatomie*'s author states it was written at university), and that he published another book soon after, continuing to publish under pseudonyms throughout his life. Unfortunately, Smedley did not publish much by way of argument supporting his theory; here we present internal evidence in the form of parallel lines of thought and expression found in several texts of the period. The book's intent is simply to generate interest and further research, not to draw final conclusions or change standing attributions. While I believe internal evidence suggests the possibility of common authorship, it may instead be taken more conservatively as indicating influences hitherto overlooked (for example, we shall see many instances where Shakespeare appears to have drawn from the books under consideration).

---

[3] Tenison, Thomas. *Baconiana, or, Certain genuine remains of Sr. Francis Bacon, Baron of Verulam, and Viscount of St. Albans in arguments civil and moral, natural, medical, theological, and bibliographical now for the first time faithfully published*. London, 1679.
[4] Vickers, Brian. "The Authenticity of Bacon's Earliest Writings." *Studies in Philology* 94, no. 2 (1997): 248-96.

Bacon's works may have been collaborative to some extent. Researchers who initially investigated the early writings of Thomas Hobbes (a sometime scribe and amanuensis for Bacon) performed two different statistical comparisons of Bacon's autograph letters and published prose, with results indicating the presence of other hands in the published works.[5] Of course, Bacon's epistolary style likely differed to his prose intended for publishing, and the polished style of the *Essays* is very different to the hastily composed *Henry VII*; but Alan Stewart, co-chair of the *Oxford Francis Bacon*, describes a scenario whereby

> surviving autograph drafts by Bacon—that is, tracts written in his own handwriting—are scant indeed, and most of them are notes, occurring in commonplace books and notebooks . . . the norm is a draft in the hand of one of Bacon's secretaries or amanuenses, with Bacon's autograph comments, often quite extensive emendations . . . That these writings range in date from 1603 to 1621 suggests that Bacon's preferred form of writing may always have been collaborative.[6]

The Workes of Benjamin Jonson (1616) is seen as a forerunner of the Shakespeare First Folio, being the first time an English playwright's works were issued in a large, expensive folio edition. Evidently it was a collaborative effort; Jonson's statement that he wrote *Volpone* "without a co-adjutor, novice, journey-man or tutor" implies that

> the main author reigned above co-adjutors (helpers or assistant writers), novices (inexperienced or probationary writers) and journeymen (writers who were newly qualified, having finished their apprenticeships). The definitions of all three positions . . . imply that each served in subservient positions to more experienced masters, such as Jonson.[7]

Scholars have been reluctant to deconstruct the Shakespeare canon into collaborations, but this attitude is beginning to change; Barry Clarke's well-researched 2019 book published by Routledge, *Francis Bacon's Contribution to Shakespeare: A New Attribution Method*, uses stylometry to argue for the presence of many hands in Shakespeare. The

---

[5] Noel B. Reynolds, G. Bruce Schaalje, John L. Hilton, "Who wrote Bacon? Assessing the respective roles of Francis Bacon and his secretaries in the production of his English works," *Literary and Linguistic Computing*, Volume 27, Issue 4, December 2012, Pages 409–425

[6] Stewart 2009.

[7] Grace Ippolo, *Dramatists and their Manuscripts in the Age of Shakespeare, Jonson, Middleton, and Heywood: Authorship, Authority and the Playhouse* (London: Routlede, 2006), p. 32.

desire to preserve the Bard as a monolithic cultural institution is understandable, however Bacon's role in the development of science gives this question greater significance, taking it outside the confines of English departments and making it universal.

Bacon and science

The first *History of the Royal Society* (1667), which records the founding of the world's oldest scientific body, depicts Bacon as *Artium Instaurator*, "Restorer of the Arts," and proclaims

> Bacon, like Moses, led us forth at last.
> The barren wilderness he past,
> Did on the very border stand
> Of the blest promis'd land,
> And from the mountain's top of his exalted wit,
> Saw it himself and shew'd us it.

Writers of the French Enlightenment revered Bacon as their inspiration; the *Encyclopédie* "owe[s] most to the Chancellor Bacon" (Diderot); "the father of the experimental philosophy" (Voltaire); "the greatest, the most universal, and the most eloquent of philosophers" (D'Alembert).[8] However, Bacon's academic reputation suffered drastically in the nineteenth and twentieth centuries; today he is often forgotten in the roll of scientific pioneers, and is rarely credited for inventing the first binary code. Bertrand Russell's *History of Western Philosophy* (1945) is typical of the prevailing tone: "Bacon's inductive method is faulty through insufficient emphasis on hypothesis"; "his philosophy is in many ways unsatisfactory"; "Bacon could have done better if he had been less concerned with worldly success." Other philosophers of science, Karl Popper and Thomas Kuhn, pretended to reject Bacon while borrowing or outright plagiarizing from him:

> I was startled to discern in the two thinkers what amounts to precisely the same project—right down to the use of precisely the same exemplum to make precisely the same points—and this despite Kuhn's determined

---

[8] Durant, Will. *The Story of Philosophy*. New York: Simon & Schuster 1926 p. 182

jettisoning of Bacon's thought from the purview of modernity and paradigmacity.[9]

Discussing the vicissitudes of Bacon's status, an editor in the ongoing sixteen-volume *Oxford Francis Bacon* wondered "Lord Verulam, once regarded as one of the greatest philosophers of the Western tradition, was relegated to an intellectual *salon des refusés* from which he has been hard put to escape. How did this state of affairs come about?"[10]

The change in Bacon's legacy began with an influential biographical essay published by Lord Macaulay in 1837. Macaulay did not attack Bacon's work—admittedly, "the most exquisitely constructed intellect that has ever been bestowed on any of the children of men"—however his motives and character were portrayed as base and callous. Many of the essay's charges were answered by James Spedding in *Evenings with a Reviewer or, A free and particular examination of Mr. Macaulay's article on Lord Bacon* (1881) and more recently by Nieves Mathews in *Francis Bacon: The History of a Character Assassination* (1996).

The historical context of Macaulay's essay is interesting for several reasons. First, *The Story of the Learned Pig*, a pamphlet printed in 1786 by one "Transmigratus," had openly stated that Bacon was behind the Shakespeare works; it was only a matter of time before the issue gained wider notice, and the authorship question eventually exploded with Delia Bacon's 1857 book *The Philosophy of Shakespeare's Plays Unfolded*. Macaulay was very likely apprised of the *Learned Pig* and remarked "the poetical faculty was powerful in Bacon's mind, but not, like his wit, so powerful as occasionally to usurp the place of his reason, and to tyrannize over the whole man." Make of that what you can.

Secondly, Macaulay wrote the article while in India serving on the Supreme Council of the colonial government; an ardent proponent of Western cultural superiority, he had written two years previously

> all the historical information which has been collected from all the books written in the Sanskrit language is less valuable than what may be found in the most paltry abridgement used at preparatory schools in England . . . a

---

[9] Desroches, Dennis. *Francis Bacon and the Limits of Scientific Knowledge*. New York: Bloomsbury Academic, 2006. p. 7. For Popper's debt to Bacon, see Urbach, Peter. *Francis Bacon's Philosophy of Science: An Account and a Reappraisal*. Lasalle, Illinois: Open Court, 1987.

[10] Rees, Graham. "Reflections on the Reputation of Francis Bacon's Philosophy." *Huntington Library Quarterly* 65, no. 3/4 (2002): 379–94

single shelf of a good European library [is] worth the whole native literature of India and Arabia.[11]

In reality, the civilizing mission of British colonialism—always to some degree a source of insecurity—was faced with an ideological challenge. Philologists had determined that Sanskrit and European languages derive from the same source; as this knowledge spread, concerns arose that the East/West divide might be seen as less definitive, and thus Britain's role in India, the crown jewel of their empire, less tenable.[12] If the Shakespeare problem was not enough, Macaulay may have regarded Bacon with additional concern because he blurs the distinction between Western "Greek rationalism" and Eastern "Oriental superstition"; this is not a widely held view of Bacon's psychological makeup, but as Macaulay himself tells us,

> In truth, much of Bacon's life was passed in a visionary world, amidst things as strange as any that are described in the Arabian Tales, or in those romances on which the curate and barber of Don Quixote's village performed so cruel an *auto-da-fe*, amidst buildings more sumptuous than the palace of Aladdin, fountains more wonderful than the golden water of Parizade, conveyances more rapid than the hippogryph of Ruggiero, arms more formidable than the lance of Astolfo, remedies more efficacious than the balsam of Fierabras.

This is a very strange passage, not only for its claim that Bacon was prone to visionary states (where did Macaulay obtain this information?) but also for its repeated hyperbolic allusions to *Don Quixote* and the *Thousand and One Nights*, the best-known example of Macaulay's much-detested Arabian literature. As a stylistic flourish it is excessive, calling attention to itself; perhaps Macaulay regretted the article and is telling us why he felt compelled to write it. In any case, he seems to be saying that while Bacon is regarded as the paragon of rational empiricism, "in truth" he had an "Eastern" or mystical side as well.

In 1657, William Rawley edited a collection of Bacon's previously unpublished speeches and miscellaneous works, entitled *Resuscitatio*. A "Life of the Honourable Author" prefixed to the book states "This lord was religious: for though the world be apt to suspect and prejudge great wits and politiques to have somewhat of the atheist, yet he was conversant with God." If anyone, Rawley was in a position to know; he

---

[11] Minute on Education, 1835
[12] McEvilley, Thomas. *The Shape of Ancient Thought: Comparative Studies in Greek and Indian Philosophies*. New York: Allworth, 2001

had been Bacon's trusted amanuensis and chaplain (later he was chaplain to Charles I and Charles II); Bacon left him £100, then a substantial sum. In recent times Bacon's writings, with their many references to God and scripture, have occasionally been interpreted as a pious cover to advance an (atheist) scientific agenda; but in fact he went so far as to state "all knowledge is to be limited by religion" and "the least part of knowledge is subject to the use for which God hath granted it, which is the benefit and relief of the state and society of man."[13]

Bacon's rumored royal lineage

Rawley's biographical sketch of Bacon was the first of its kind in English; previously a similar thing had appeared in Pierre Amboise's *Histoire Naturelle de Mre. Francois Bacon* (1631). Amboise wrote that Bacon was "born in the purple and brought up with the expectation of a great career," purple of course being the color reserved for royalty. Rawley begins his account

> Francis Bacon, the glory of his age and nation, the adorner and ornament of learning, was born in York House, or York Place, in the Strand, on the two and twentieth day of January, in the year of our Lord 1560 [1561].

The question of Bacon's birthplace, whether York House or York Place, imports more than might appear; York House was the London home of Sir Nicholas and Lady Anne Bacon, next door stood York Place or the palace of Whitehall, main residence of Queen Elizabeth and Robert Dudley, the Earl of Leicester. At the time, a rumor that Elizabeth was pregnant bruited abroad; in August of 1560 one Anne Dowe of Brentwood, a sixty-eight-year-old widow, was the first of several arrested for speaking thus publicly. Soon after, the Spanish ambassador met with William Cecil, Elizabeth's chief counselor (soon to be Francis Bacon's uncle), and wrote of the encounter

> [Cecil] said that the Queen was going on so strangely that he was about to withdraw from her service ... Lord Robert had made himself master of the business of the state and of the person of the Queen, to the extreme injury of the realm, with the intention of marrying her, and she herself was shutting herself up in the palace to the peril of her health and life. That the realm would tolerate the marriage, he said he did not believe ... Last of all,

---

[13] *Valerius Terminus, or Of the Interpretation of Nature* (~1603)

> he said that they were thinking of destroying Lord Robert's wife. They had given out that she was ill, but she was not ill at all; she was very well and taking care not to be poisoned... Since writing the above, I hear the Queen has published the death of Robert's wife.[14]

Amy Dudley was found at their home near Oxford with a broken neck. Dudley did not attend the funeral and the court ruled it an accident; four months later, Francis Bacon was born.

Writers who ascribe the Shakespeare works to Bacon often claim he was the son of Elizabeth and Dudley, and that the couple had another son, Robert Devereaux, the Earl of Essex, born four years later. Before the possibility of such outrageous fortune is dismissed out of hand, it is worth reflecting that it would help explain the emotional power of *Hamlet* and *Macbeth*, otherwise thought to have originated in Shakespeare's imagination. Bacon has been criticized for his prosecution of Essex, his friend and patron, for treason in 1601; this was one of Macaulay's principal points of attack. But if Bacon and Essex had the same parents, it would mean Francis Bacon was born of a "virgin," a born king (but as it turned out, not of this world—his library was dukedom enough), and he prosecuted his rebellious brother who attempted to take the throne by force. Perhaps an awareness of these parallels with Jesus gave Bacon the boldness to proclaim that he was more than a man:

> Now if the utility of any single invention so moved men, that they accounted more than man him who could include the whole human race in some solitary benefit, that invention is certainly much more exalted, which by a kind of mastery contains within itself all particular inventions, and delivers the mind from bondage, and opens it a road, that under sure and unerring guidance it may penetrate to whatever can be of novelty and further advancement.[15]

Bacon's unorthodox biography also parallels certain features of the mythological hero archetype outlined in Otto Rank's *Myth of the Birth of the Hero* (1909) and Freud's *Moses and Monotheism* (1939): conception in secret, royal birth attended with grave difficulties, adoption by those of a lesser station, fears that the child will be a danger to the state. These similarities are the more striking, as the myths deal with an abandoned prince who returns to overcome his father, and Bacon gave us modern

---

[14] Letter to the Duchess of Parma, dated 11 September 1560

[15] *Thoughts concerning the Interpretation of Nature*, Tr. Basil Montagu *The Works of Francis Bacon* London: William Pickering 1834

science, the tool with which humanity challenges our common Father. Rank, like Freud, questioned the authorship of the Shakespeare works, and in *Art and Artist* (1932) he conjectured (without noting that *Hamlet* was published just after Elizabeth died):

> about Shakespeare, it seems to me not improbable that the inspired poet portrayed himself in the Danish prince, so that he might with impunity utter high treason . . . the participation of Hamlet in his entrapping play might be explained from the fact that powerful opponents of Elizabeth did really use the poet as a means to attack her and stir her conscience. In this case, we should have a reflection, in Hamlet's editing of the "play," of the part important friends of the poet actually had in his work.[16]

The Story of the Learned Pig contains a subtle allusion to Bacon's royal descent, plainly stating he was behind the Shakespeare works.

> My parents, indeed, were of low extraction; my mother sold fish about the streets of this metropolis, and my father was a water-carrier celebrated by Ben Jonson in his comedy of *Every Man in his Humour* . . . I soon after contracted a friendship with that great man and first of geniuses, the 'Immortal Shakespeare,' and am happy in now having it in my power to refuse the prevailing opinion of his having run his country for deer-stealing, which is as false as it is disgracing. The fact is, Sir, that he had contracted an intimacy with the wife of a country Justice near Stratford, from his having extolled her beauty in a common ballad; and was unfortunately, by his worship himself, detected in a very awkward situation with her. Shakespeare, to avoid the consequences of this discovery, thought it most prudent to decamp. This I had from his own mouth. With equal falsehood has he been father'd with many spurious dramatic pieces. *Hamlet*, *Othello*, *As You Like It*, the *Tempest*, and *Midsummer's Night Dream*, for five; of all which I confess myself to be the author.

While the *Learned Pig* does not specifically mention Bacon by name, the "water-carrier celebrated by Ben Jonson" is a character named Cob; when he appears onstage the following exchange takes place:

> *Cob.* I sir, I and my linage ha' kept a poor house, here, in our days.
> *Mat.* **Thy linage, Monsieur Cob, what linage, what linage?**
> *Cob.* Why Sir, **an ancient linage, and a princely. Mine ance'try came from a King's belly, no worse Man**
> . . .

---

[16] Rank, Otto. *The Myth of the Birth of the Hero and Other Essays.* New York: Vintage, 1959 p. 236-7

> *Cob.* I Sir, with favour of your Worship's nose, Mr. Matthew, why not the ghost of a herring Cob, as well as the ghost of **rasher-bacon**?
> *Mat.* **Roger Bacon**, thou wouldst say?
> *Cob.* I say **Rasher-Bacon**. They were both broil'd o' the coals; and a man may smell broil'd meat, I hope? you are a scholar, upsolve me that, now…
> …
> *Mat.* Lie in a water-bearer's House! A Gentleman of his havings! Well, I'll tell him my mind.

Bacon was born in the sign of Aquarius, or the house of the water bearer; here it might be worthwhile to cite the oldest representative of the heroic archetype, Sargon of Akkad, founder of Babylon:

> Sargon, the mighty king, King of Agade, am I. My mother was a vestal, my father I knew not, while my father's brother dwelt in the mountains. In my city Azuripani, which is situated on the bank of the Euphrates, my mother, the vestal, bore me. In a hidden place she brought me forth. She laid me in a vessel made of reeds, closed my door with pitch, and dropped me down into the river, which did not drown me. The river carried me to Akki, the water carrier. Akki the water carrier lifted me up in the kindness of his heart, Akki the water carrier raised me as his own son, Akki the water carrier raised me as his own son, Akki the water carrier made of me his gardener. In my work as a gardener I was beloved by Ishtar, I became the king, and for forty-five years I held kingly sway.

In the *Advancement of Learning* Bacon speaks of "enigmatical" writing "to remove the vulgar capacities from being admitted to the secrets of knowledges, and to reserve them to selected auditors, or wits of such sharpness as can pierce the veil." Again, in *Valerius Terminus*,

> the discretion anciently observed … of publishing in a manner whereby it shall not be to the capacity nor taste of all, but shall as it were single and adopt his reader, is not to be laid aside, both for the avoiding of abuse in the excluded, and the strengthening of affection in the admitted.

Bacon invited future generations of readers, his "true sons of knowledge," to carry on his tradition of the lamp (*traditio lampadis*) and investigate his works more thoroughly; for

> the glory of God is to conceal a thing, but the glory of the king is to find it out, as if according to the innocent play of children the divine Majesty took delight to hide his works, to the end to have them found out…

A DISCOVRSE VPON THE MEANES OF VVEL GOVERNING AND MAINTAINING IN GOOD PEACE, A KINGDOME, OR OTHER PRINCIPALITIE.

Divided into three parts, namely, The Counsell, the Religion, and the Policie, vvhich a Prince ought to hold and follow.

Againſt *Nicholas Machiavell* the Florentine.

Tranſlated into Engliſh by Simon Patericke.

LONDON,
Printed by Adam Iſlip.
1602.

1. *Anti-Machiavel*

> What at first appears to be their "philosophy of life" sometimes turns out to be only a felicitous but shameless lifting of a passage from almost any author . . . [Shakespeare] has his Montaigne, his Seneca, and his Machiavelli, or his Anti-Machiavelli like the others.
>
> T.S. Eliot, Introduction to *The Wheel of Fire* (1949)

Voltaire likened Bacon's *Novum Organum* (1620) to a scaffold which enabled the edifice of modern science to be built, remarking that of Bacon's works, "at this time [it] is the most useless and the least read," for "when the edifice was built, part of it at least, the scaffold was no longer of service."[17] Bacon's intervention challenged the prevailing epistemology of Aristotle's *Organon* (deduction or the syllogism, a top-down method which starts with a premise assumed to be true universally) and instead suggested induction, a bottom-up method of establishing truth progressively:

> There are and can be only two ways of searching into and discovering truth. The one flies from the senses and particulars to the most general axioms, and from these principles, the truth of which it takes for settled and immovable, proceeds to judgment and middle axioms . . . The other derives axioms from the senses and particulars, rising by a gradual and unbroken ascent, so that it arrives at the most general axioms last of all; which is the true but unattempted way.

In other words, as he wrote earlier in *The Advancement of Learning*, "if a man will begin with certainties, he shall end in doubts; but if he will be content to begin with doubts he shall end in certainties." Curiously, in 1576, the year Bacon left Cambridge, an anonymous writer began his rebuttal of Machiavelli with similar material:

> Aristotle and other philosophers teach us, and experience confirms, that there are two ways to come unto the knowledge of things. The one, when from the causes and maxims, men come to knowledge of the effects and consequences. The other, when contrary, by the effects and consequences we come to know the causes and maxims... The first of these ways is proper and peculiar unto the mathematicians, who teach the truth of their theorems and problems by their demonstrations drawn from maxims,

---

[17] *Philosophical Letters*, 1733

which are common sentences allowed of themselves for true by the common sense and judgment of all men. The second way belongs to other sciences, as to natural philosophy, moral philosophy, physic, law, policy, and other sciences, whereof the knowledge proceeds more commonly by a resolute order of effects to their causes, and from particulars to general maxims.

Published in French at Geneva, *Anti-Machiavel* went through twenty-four printings in five languages and was quite influential in its time. It is attributed to Innocent Gentillet, a French Huguenot lawyer who fled to Geneva after the St. Bartholomew massacres in 1572, however a bibliographer questioned its authorship as early as 1584: "For my part, I believe that all these Gentillets are masks, and that the author of *Anti-Machiavel* is not known."[18] Beginning with the 1577 Latin translation, the book bears a dedication "for kinred" to Francis Hastings and Edward Bacon (half-brother of Francis Bacon), then living in Geneva.

TO THE MOST FAMOVS YONG
GENTLEMEN, AS WELL FOR RELIGION, MODESTIE, AND OTHER VERTVES, AS AL-
so for kinred, *Francis Hastings*, and *Edward Bacon*, most heartie salutations.

The dedication exhorts Edward to

> imitate the wisdom, sanctimony, and integrity of your Father, the right Honorable Lord Nicholas Bacon, Keeper of the broad Seal of England, a man right renowned; that you may lively express the image of your Father's virtues in the excellent towardness which you naturally have from your most virtuous Father.[19]

---

[18] *Les bibliothèques françoises de La Croix du Maine et de Du Verdier*, volume I, p. 220. Paris: Saillant & Nyon, 1772.
[19] The anonymous author of the *Arte of English Poesie* (1589), which bears a dedication to Francis Bacon's uncle Lord Burghley, was also intimately familiar with Sir

The dedication opens with a story from Plutarch about the Greek statesman Solon talking with Thespis, the poet and actor for whom thespians are named:

> After Solon had seen Thespis' first edition and action of a tragedy, and meeting with him before the play, he asked if he was not ashamed to publish such feigned fables under so noble, yet a counterfeit personage. Thespis answered that it was no disgrace upon a stage, merrily and in sport, to say and do anything. Then Solon, striking hard upon the earth with his staff, replied thus: "Yea but shortly, we that now like and embrace this play, shall find it practiced in our contracts and common affairs." This man of deep understanding saw that public discipline and reformation of manners, attempted once in sport and jest, would soon quail; and corruption, at the beginning passing in play, would fall and end in earnest.

Bacon shared this concern with the pedagogy of the stage, as expressed in *The Advancement of Learning*:

> Dramatic poesy, which has the theatre for its world, would be of excellent use if well directed. For the stage is capable of no small influence both of discipline and of corruption. Now of corruptions in this kind we have enough; but the discipline has in our times been plainly neglected. And though in modern states play-acting is esteemed but as a toy, except when it is too satirical and biting, yet among the ancients it was used as a means of educating men's minds to virtue.

The same thought is also found in *Don Quixote*, which we will visit later:

> Seeing the comedy, as Tully affirms, ought to be a mirror of man's life, a pattern of manners, and an image of truth, those that are now exhibited are mirrors of vanity, patterns of folly, and images of voluptuousness.

Hamlet also refers to the theatre as a mirror: "anything so overdone is from the purpose of playing, whose end, both at the first and now, was and is to hold, as 'twere, the mirror up to nature."

Events rehearsed in *Anti-Machiavel* are depicted in many of Shakespeare's English and Roman history plays, and allusions to the book in works with early references to Shakespeare, *Greene's Groatsworth of Wit* (1592) and *Polimantiea* (1595) have been noted previously by scholars.

Nicholas: "I have come to the Lord Keeper Sir Nicholas Bacon, and found him sitting in his gallery alone with the works of Quintilian before him; indeed, he was a most eloquent man, and of rare learning and wisdom, as ever I knew England to breed, and one that joyed as much in learned men and men of good wits."

Echoes of *Anti-Machiavel* have been found in *Measure for Measure*,[20] and *Hamlet* may have been influenced by a passage which includes incest on the part of the emperor Claudius, poisoning, and improper royal succession:

> When the emperor Claudius would espouse Agrippina, his brother's daughter, he made a law whereby he authorized the marriage of the uncle with the niece, which was published all over . . . indeed this marriage fell out not well for him; for Agrippina poisoned him to bring Nero to the empire, her son by another marriage; although Claudius had by his first wife Messalina a natural son called Brittanicus, whom Nero poisoned when he came to the empire. So that by the incestuous marriage wherewith Claudius had contaminated and poisoned his house, he and his natural son, who by reason should have been his successor, were killed with poison.

Concerning Machiavelli's advice to be both man and beast, lion and fox, *Anti-Machiavel* wondered "should we call this beastliness or malice, what Machiavelli says of Chiron? Or has he read that Chiron was both a man and a beast? Who has told him that he was delivered to Achilles to teach him that goodly knowledge to be both a man and a beast?" Shakespeare's *Timon of Athens* displays similar impatience with Machiavelli's advice:

> A beastly ambition, which the gods grant thee t'
> attain to! If thou wert the lion, the fox would
> beguile thee; if thou wert the lamb, the fox would
> eat three: if thou wert the fox, the lion would
> suspect thee . . . What beast couldst thou be, that
> were not subject to a beast? and what a beast art
> thou already, that seest not thy loss in
> transformation!

Bacon's *Advancement of Learning*:

> Achilles was brought up under Chiron the Centaur, who was part a man and part a beast: expounded ingeniously but corruptly by Machiavel, that it belongeth to the education and discipline of princes to know as well how to play the part of the lion in violence and the fox in guile

Another parallel is found in *The Rape of Lucrece*:

> For princes are the glass, the school, the book,

---

[20] Holland, Norman N. "Measure for Measure: The Duke and the Prince." *Comparative Literature* 11, no. 1 (1959): 16–20.

Where subjects' eyes do learn, do read, do look.

Anti-Machiavel:

> commonly (said Herodian) men imitate their prince and give themselves to such things as the prince loves . . . whenever a prince is soft and clement, there is no doubt but his subjects will imitate him therein; for it is the people's nature to conform themselves unto their prince's manners, as the proverb says:
>
>> The example of the prince's life in all things commonly
>> The subject seeks to imitate with all his possibility.

The Anatomie of the Minde, also 1576, which we will visit in the next chapter:

> Truly and commonly is it said . . . such prince, such people, such superiors, such subjects . . . men frame themselves and conform their manners as they see others placed in chief seat of authority, as it were to the view and sight of all men.

An allusion with multiple parallels occurs in *The Advancement of Learning*:

> As for evil arts, if a man would set down for himself that principle of Machiavel, that "a man seek not to attain virtue itself, but the appearance only thereof; because the credit of virtue is a help, but the use of it is cumber"; or that other of his principles, that "he presuppose that men are not fitly to be wrought otherwise but by fear, and therefore that he seek to have every man obnoxious, low, and in strait," which the Italians call *seminar spine*, to sow thorns: or that other principle, contained in the verse which Cicero citeth, *Cadant amici, dummodo inimici intercidant* [Let friends fall, provided our enemies perish with them], as the Triumvirs, which sold every one to other the lives of their friends for the deaths of their enemies: or that other protestation of L. Catilina, to set on fire and trouble states, to the end to fish in droumy waters, and to unwrap their fortunes.

Anti-Machiavel relates the story of "Catiline, who with his companions went about to destroy his country with fire and sword"; twice uses the phrase "fish in troubled waters," and devotes a chapter to the policy of keeping subjects poor. It also speaks of Cicero's death being procured by trade:

> Antony, to have his enemy Cicero (whom Octavian favored as his friend), was content to deliver in exchange Lucius Caesar, his own uncle on his

mother's side; so that the one was exchanged for the other, and they both died ... Is it not a strange thing to hear that a friend should be betrayed to death, to have the cruel pleasure of slaying an enemy? Yet by this course died a hundred and thirty senators, besides many other persons of quality.

This brutal bargaining is depicted in *Julius Caesar*:

Octavius. Prick him down, Antony.
Lepidus. Upon condition Publius shall not live,
Who is your sister's son, Mark Antony.
Antony. He shall not live; look, with a spot I damn him.

Two scenes later, we learn that Cicero is one of the victims:

Brutus. Therein our letters do not well agree;
Mine speak of seventy senators that died
By their prescription, Cicero being one.

The first edition of *Anti-Machiavel* was dedicated to Duke of Alençon, brother of Henri III and heir to the French throne (Machiavelli had dedicated *The Prince* to Alençon's grandfather, Lorenzo de Medici). In September of 1575, Alençon joined with Huguenot forces opposed to the Catholic crown; his *Protestation*, calling for reforms and an end to foreign influence at court, was published in Geneva by Gentillet, who subsequently printed his own response to Alençon's appeal. In 1583 Alençon disastrously tried to attack Antwerp under the color of amity; when Shakespeare called his ancestor in *1 Henry VI* "that notorious Machiavel," adding "take this compact of a truce/Although you break it when your pleasure serves," he was alluding to the more recent duke's maneuvers. *Shakespeare's Answer to Machiavelli* notes "the only two times the world "Machiavel" is uttered in the history plays, it is spoken first by Richard York and second by his true son, Richard Gloucester [Richard III]."[21] York is himself Machiavellian, deriding "churchlike humours [that] fits not for a crown"; but Shakespeare tells us that the father, who "will hunt this deer to death," is surpassed in perfidy by the son, who "must hunt this wolf to death." In *2 Henry VI* the latter says "Priests pray for enemies, but princes kill." In *3 Henry VI* he says

I can add colours to the chameleon,
Change shapes with Proteus for advantages,

---

[21] Hollingshead, Stephen. *Shakespeare's Answer to Machiavelli: The Role of the Christian Prince in the History Plays*. Diss., Marquette University, 1996.

And set the murderous Machiavel to school.

Anti-Machiavel:

> as soon as the prince shall clothe himself with Proteus' garments, and has no hold nor certitude of his word, nor in his actions, men may well say that his malady is incurable, and that in all vices he has taken the nature of the chameleon

Proteus and the chameleon were frequently paired following the popular *Adages* of Erasmus; an entry in Francis Bacon's *Promus*, a collection of proverbs and quips, reads "Chameleon, Proteus, Euripus" (Euripus is a strait in the Aegean with currents that regularly reverse direction). Shakespeare's *Two Gentlemen of Verona*, which features a character named Proteus, twice refers to the chameleon.

Bacon's *History of the Reign of King Henry VII* echoes both Shakespeare and *Anti-Machiavel* in its characterization of Richard III:

> Richard, the third of that name, king in fact only, but tyrant both in title and regiment, and so commonly termed and reputed in all times since, was by the Divine Revenge, favouring the design of an exiled man, overthrown and slain at Bosworth Field; there succeeded in the kingdom the Earl of Richmond, thenceforth styled Henry the Seventh.

Anti-Machiavel's account states "A similar punishment happened by the judgment of God to that cruel king Richard of England." Divine intervention against Richard III was frequently stressed because the Tudor dynasty's claim to the throne rested on his usurpation; Shakespeare's *Richard III* strongly emphasized this line: "Bloody thou art, bloody will be thy end"; "O God . . . revenge his death!"; "heav'n with lightning strike the murd'rer dead," etc.

The Great Assizes holden in Parnassus (1645, attributed to George Wither) features a court of poets and scholars, with Francis Bacon as Chancellor of Parnassus, before whom are arraigned authors charged with "strange abuses, committed against [Apollo] and the Nine Muses":

> He was accused, that he had used his skill,
> Parnassus with strange heresies to fill,
> And that he labour'd had for to bring in,
> Th' exploded doctrines of the Florentine,
> And taught that to dissemble and to lie,
> Were vital parts of humane policy.

"Th' exploded doctrines of the Florentine" can only refer to *Anti-Machiavel*. The court of Parnassus also includes William Shakespeare as "Writer of weekly accounts," Ben Jonson as "Keeper of the Trophonian Den," and the scholar Isaac Casaubon, a friend of Bacon's who was born in Geneva to Huguenot refugee parents. Casaubon is best known for proving that the *Corpus Hermeticum* dates from the Common Era; in a later chapter we will discuss Bacon's possible role in some of the Hermetic literature of his time. Bacon wrote in a letter to Casaubon: "to write at leisure that which is to be read at leisure matters little; but to bring about the better ordering of man's life and business, with all its troubles and difficulties, by the help of sound and true contemplations—this is the thing I am at."[22]

Much has been written about Machiavelli's influence on Francis Bacon; the two are frequently mentioned together, and to some extent their names have been fused in the public mind. More often than not, however, when alluding to Machiavelli Bacon is actually adverting to *Anti-Machiavel*; in over fifty places his writings, speeches, and letters parallel the earlier book dedicated "for kinred" to his half-brother. Several professors have at least suggested a connection; Sydney Anglo remarked that *Anti-Machiavel*'s "appeals to historical exemplars are really no more rigid, and no further removed from true inductive reasoning, than is Machiavelli's use of Livy."[23] Another writer said "it may not have been mere coincidence that in his account of the Essex trial . . . Francis Bacon echoes Gentillet in his conclusion that ambition engenders treason and treason finally brings the complete ruin of the traitor."[24] Nigel Bawcutt seems impatient with the book's obscurity:

> Now it might be helpful to scholars if it could be conclusively proved that they need not bother to read Gentillet's long and sometimes tedious book, but unfortunately this is not the case, and one of the points to be made in this article is that scholars who are ignorant of Gentillet may fail to recognize allusions to him if they should encounter them.[25]

---

[22] Spedding, James. *The Letters and the Life of Francis Bacon, Vol. IV*, p. 147. London: Longman, Green, Reader, and Dyer, 1868.
[23] Anglo, Sydney. "The Reception of Machiavelli in Tudor England: A Re-Assessment." *Il Politico* 31, no. 1 (1966): 127-38.
[24] Zaharia, Alis. "Circulating Texts in the Renaissance: Simon Patericke's Translation of Anti-Machiavel and the Fortunes of Gentillet in England." *The University of Bucharest Review* vol. IV, no. 1 (2014): 54-62.
[25] Bawcutt, N. W. "The 'Myth of Gentillet' Reconsidered: An Aspect of Elizabethan Machiavellianism." *The Modern Language Review* 99, no. 4 (2004): 863–74.

Could Francis Bacon have written a lengthy book of political philosophy, in French, at fifteen—perhaps fourteen? He invented the first binary code in his teens, and as Macaulay said, "while yet a boy he was plunged into the midst of diplomatic business"; "his gigantic scheme of philosophical reform is said by some writers to have been planned before he was fifteen." Pascal wrote a treatise on vibrating bodies at age nine; William Cullen Bryant published a book of satiric political verse at thirteen; Melanchthon wrote his *Rudiments of the Greek Language* at eleven or twelve, and Agrippa d'Aubigne translated Plato's *Crito* at ten.

But is it possible that Bacon, at fifteen, could have caused a book to be published at Geneva? Possibly; he was in France at the time, and his family had close connections to the city going back to Anne Bacon's father, Sir Anthony Cooke, who corresponded with Calvin and met Theodore Beza, Calvin's successor in Geneva, while living on the continent as a Protestant exile during the reign of Mary I.[26] Beza approved *Anti-Machiavel* for publication; in 1580-81 Anthony Bacon lodged with Beza, and in 1582 Beza dedicated his *Meditations* to Anne Bacon. Antonio D'Andrea attributes the 1577 *Anti-Machiavel* dedication to Beza or Lambert Daneau,[27] a Huguenot theologian who was also a tutor of Francis and Anthony Bacon; in 1586 Daneau dedicated his commentary on the minor prophets to Anthony.[28]

Bacon's family motto *mediocria firma* ("moderation is stable" or "the middle way is sure") is flatly contradicted by Machiavelli, who complained "men take certain middle ways that are very harmful, for they do not know how to be altogether wicked or altogether good." This is handled in *Anti-Machiavel* and in Bacon's *Wisdom of the Ancients*:

> Mediocrity, or the middle way, is most commended in moral actions; in contemplative sciences not so celebrated, though no less profitable and commodious; but in political employments to be used with great heed and judgment . . . The way of virtue lies in a direct path between excess and defect

---

[26] McIntosh, Marjorie Keniston. "Sir Anthony Cooke: Tudor Humanist, Educator, and Religious Reformer." *Proceedings of the American Philosophical Society* 119, no. 3 (1975): 233-50.
[27] D'Andrea, Antonio. "Machiavelli, Satan, and the Gospel." *Yearbook of Italian Studies* (1971): 156-77.
[28] Vickers, Brian. *Francis Bacon: The Major Works*, p. 562. Oxford: Oxford University Press, 1996.

This idea is also found in *Merchant of Venice*: "It is no mean happiness, therefore, to be seated in the mean."

Machiavelli counseled a prince "to appear merciful, faithful, humane, religious, upright, and to be so, but with a mind so framed that should you require not to be so, you may be able and know how to change to the opposite." Bacon wrote "constancy is the foundation on which virtues rest," echoing *Anti-Machiavel*: "constancy is a quality which ordinarily accompanies all other virtues; it is, as it were, of their substance and nature." This idea is also found in *Measure for Measure*: "it is virtuous to be constant in any undertaking"; and *Two Gentlemen of Verona* (spoken by Proteus): "were man but constant, here were perfect."

Machiavelli's assertion that "when the deed accuses, the effect excuses," commonly interpreted as "the ends justify the means," is challenged in *Anti-Machiavel* and strongly condemned in one of Bacon's prosecution speeches: "evil is never in order towards good. So that it is plainly to make God the author of evil, and to say with those that St. Paul speaketh of, Let us do evil that good may come thereof, of whom the Apostle says excellently *That their damnation is just*." I will here note by the way what appears to be an intentional misprint in the 1606 English edition of Jean Bodin's *Six Books of a Commonwealth*, which reads: "Frauncis Machiauell, and many others following Polybius, have as it were with one consent approved his opinion."

Thus the relationship between Machiavelli and Bacon is more complex than has hitherto been assumed, and might be summarized in what has been said of Shakespeare: "while he clearly rejects the most fundamental tenets of Machiavellian political philosophy as unnatural and therefore destructive, he is not so foolish as to dismiss Machiavelli's other insights out of hand."[29]

Parallelisms

Bacon, *Advancement of Learning*:

As for evil arts, if a man would set down for himself that principle of Machiavel, "That a man seek not to attain virtue itself, but the appearance only thereof; because the credit of virtue is a help, but the use of it is cumber"... or that other protestation of L. Catilina, to set on

---

[29] Hollingshead, 1996.

fire and trouble states, to the end to fish in droumy waters, and to unwrap their fortunes

Anti-Machiavel:

As for peace, these people never like it, for they always fish in troubled water, gathering riches and heaps of the treasures of the realm while it is in trouble and confusion

We should not then see France to be governed and ruled by strangers, as it is; we should not feel the calamities and troubles of civil wars and dissentions, which they enterprise to maintain their greatness and magnitude, and to fish in troubled water

~

Bacon, *Advancement of Learning*:

Machiavel had reason to put the question, "which is the more ungrateful towards the well-deserving, the prince or the people?" though he accuses both of ingratitude. The thing does not proceed wholly from the ingratitude either of princes or people; but it is generally attended with the envy of the nobility; who secretly repine at the event, though happy and prosperous, because it was not procured by themselves

Anti-Machiavel:

But I must say that sometimes such changes have been procured upon envy, rather than upon just complaint against those who governed; and such envies often proceed when kings govern themselves by men of base hand, as they call them, for then princes and great lords are jealous

~

Bacon, "Of Seditions and Troubles":

Also, as Machiavel noteth well, when princes, that ought to be common parents, make themselves as a party, and lean to a side, it is as a boat that is overthrown by uneven weight on the one side… For when the authority of princes is made but an accessary to a cause, and that there be other bands that tie faster than the band of sovereignty, kings begin to be put almost out of possession

Anti-Machiavel:

For if he nourishes partialities among his subjects, he cannot possibly carry himself so equally towards both parties, but in them both will be jealousy and suspicion. Each party will esteem the other to be more favored, whereupon he will hate his prince, and by that means it may come to pass that the prince shall be hated by both parties; and so both the one and the other shall machinate his ruin, which he can hardly shun, having all their evil wills

~

Bacon, *Advancement of Learning*:

But that opinion I may condemn with like reason as Machiavel doth that other, that moneys were the sinews of wars; whereas (saith he) the true sinews of the wars are the sinews of men's arms, that is, a valiant, populous, and military nation; and he voucheth aptly the authority of Solon, who when Croesus shewed him his treasury of gold said to him, that if another came that had better iron he would be master of his gold

Anti-Machiavel:

And although Machiavelli in a certain place where he speaks of war, maintains that the common saying is false, that money is the sinews of war; this hinders not, but what we say may be true

The great treasures of king Croesus of Lydia incited him to war against king Cyrus of Persia and Media, to his own destruction

~

Bacon, *Advancement of Learning*:

So in the fable that Achilles was brought up under Chiron the Centaur, who was part a man and part a beast: expounded ingeniously but corruptly by Machiavel, that it belongeth to the education and discipline of princes to know as well how to play the part of the lion in violence and the fox in guile, as of the man in virtue and justice

Anti-Machiavel:

But should we call this beastliness or malice, what Machiavelli says of Chiron? Or has he read that Chiron was both a man and a beast? Who has told him that he was delivered to Achilles to teach him that goodly knowledge to be both a man and a beast?

~

Bacon, *Advancement of Learning*:

Concerning want, and that it is the case of learned men usually to begin with little and not to grow rich so fast as other men, by reason they convert not their labours chiefly to lucre and increase; it were good to leave the common place in commendation of poverty to some friar to handle, to whom much was attributed by Machiavel in this point, when he said, that "the kingdom of the clergy had been long before at an end, if the reputation and reverence towards the poverty of friars had not borne out the scandal of the superfluities and excesses of bishops and prelates"

Anti-Machiavel:

These mendicants then, being obliged and restrained unto poverty by a solemn vow which they made at their profession in their orders, they are so annexed, united, and incorporated in it and with it, that never after they could be never so little separated or dismembered, what diligence or labor soever they used to do it. Hereof they have found themselves much troubled and sorrowful, for howsoever gallant and goodly the *Theorique* of Poverty is, yet in practice they have found it a little too difficult and hard

~

Bacon, *Advancement of Learning*:

And therefore the form of writing which of all others is fittest for this variable argument of negotiation and occasions is that which Machiavel chose wisely and aptly for government; namely, discourse upon histories or examples… And it hath much greater life for practice when the discourse attendeth upon the example, than when the example attendeth upon the discourse. For this is no point of order, as it seemeth at first, but of substance. For when the example is the ground, being set down in an history at large, it is set down with all circumstances, which may sometimes control the discourse thereupon made and sometimes supply it, as a very pattern for action; whereas the examples alleged for the discourse's sake are cited succinctly and without particularity, and carry a servile aspect toward the discourse which they are brought in to make good

Anti-Machiavel:

Yet although the maxims and general rules of the political art may somewhat serve to know well to guide and govern a public estate, whether a principality or free city, yet they cannot be so certain as the maxims of the mathematicians, but are rules rather very dangerous, yea pernicious if men cannot make them serve and apply them unto affairs as they happen to come; and not to apply the affairs unto these maxims and rules. For the circumstances, dependencies, consequences, and antecedents of every affair and particular business, are all for the most part diverse and contrary; so that although two affairs be like, yet men must not therefore conduct and determine them by one same rule or maxim, because of the diversity and difference of accidents and circumstances

~

Bacon, *Novum Organum*:

There are and can be only two ways of searching into and discovering truth. The one flies from the senses and particulars to the most general axioms, and from these principles, the truth of which it takes for settled and immovable, proceeds to judgment and middle axioms. And this way is now in fashion. The other derives axioms from the senses and particulars, rising by a gradual and unbroken ascent, so that it arrives at the most general axioms last of all

Anti-Machiavel:

Aristotle and other philosophers teach us, and experience confirms, that there are two ways to come unto the knowledge of things. The one, when from the causes and maxims, men come to knowledge of the effects and consequences. The other, when contrary, by the effects and consequences we come to know the causes and maxims… The first of these ways is proper and peculiar unto the mathematicians, who teach the truth of their theorems and problems by their demonstrations drawn from maxims, which are common sentences allowed of themselves for true by the common sense and judgment of all men. The second way belongs to other sciences, as to natural philosophy, moral philosophy, physic, law, policy, and other sciences

Bacon, "Of Discourse":

It is good, in discourse and speech of conversation, to vary and intermingle speech of the present occasion with arguments, tales with reasons, asking of questions with telling of opinions, and jest with earnest

Anti-Machiavel:

For as Cato says, amongst serious things joyous and merry things would be sometimes mixed

Bacon, *New Atlantis*:

The reverence of a man's self is, next religion, the chiefest bridle of all vices

Anti-Machiavel:

Behold then the consequence of that most wicked and detestable doctrine of that wicked atheist; which is to bring all people to a spite and a mockery of God and his religion, and of all holy things, and to let go the bridle to all vices and villainies

Bacon, *De augmentis scientiarum*:

Constancy is the foundation on which virtues rest.

Anti-Machiavel:

I will then presuppose that constancy is a quality which ordinarily accompanies all other virtues; it is, as it were, of their substance and nature

Bacon, "Of Adversity":

Prosperity doth best discover vice, but adversity doth best discover virtue

Anti-Machiavel:

Adversity also is a true touchstone to prove who are feigned or true friends, for when a man feels labyrinths of troubles fall on him, dissembling friends depart from him, and those who are good abide with him, as said the poet Euripides: Adversity the best and certain'st friends doth get, prosperity both good and evil alike doth fit

∼

Bacon, "Of Great Place":

It is much true which was anciently spoken: A place showeth the man, and it showeth some to the better, and some to the worse

Anti-Machiavel:

And we see but too much by experience that the old proverb is true, honors change manners

∼

Bacon, "Of Suspicion":

But this would not be done to men of base natures; for they, if they find themselves once suspected, will never be true

Anti-Machiavel:

For the best fortress that is, is not to be thought evil by subjects; and if a prince is once thought so, there is no fortress that can save him

∼

Bacon, *Apophthegms New and Old*:

Mr. Bettenham used to say, that riches were like muck: when it lay upon an heap, it gave a stench, and ill odour; but when it was spread upon the ground, then it was the cause of much fruit

Bacon, "Of Riches":

Of great riches there is no real use, except it be in the distribution; the rest is but conceit

Anti-Machiavel:

Briefly, it is neither good nor profitable for a prince to heap up great treasures and riches enclosed in one place. And what then? must a sovereign prince be poor? No, but contrary, he has need to be rich and very opulent, for otherwise he shall be feeble and weak, and cannot make head against his enemies; but his riches and treasures must be in the purses and houses of his subjects

~

Bacon, "Of Riches":

Men leave their riches either to their kindred, or to the public; and moderate portions prosper best in both. A great state left to an heir, is as a lure to all the birds of prey round about to seize on him, if he be not the better stablished in years and judgment

Anti-Machiavel:

For it is neither good nor profitable that a prince treasures up heaps of riches; for it serves for a bait to draw unto him enemies, or to engender quarrels and divisions after him; and we often see that princes' great treasures are causes of more evil than good

~

Bacon, *Advancement of Learning*:

It is true, that taxes levied by public consent, less dispirit, and sink the minds of the subject, than those imposed in absolute governments

Anti-Machiavel:

It is certain that a prince may well make war and impose taxes without the consent of his subjects, by an absolute power; but it is better for him to use his civil power, so should he be better obeyed

~

Anti-Machiavel:

true charity is joined unto faith, pity, and all other virtues

Bacon, *Advancement of Learning*:

But these be heathen and profane passages, having but a shadow of that divine state of mind which religion and the holy faith doth conduct men unto, by imprinting upon their souls Charity, which is excellently called the bond of Perfection, because it comprehendeth and fasteneth all virtues together

Anti-Machiavel:

But I must say that the Christian religion has launched and entered far deeper into the doctrine of good manners than the pagans and philosophers have done. For proof hereof I will take the maxim of Plato, that we are not only born for ourselves, but that our birth is partly for our country, partly for our parents, and partly for our friends. Behold a goodly sentence we can say no other; but if we compare it with the doctrine of Christians, it will be found maimed and defective. For what mention does Plato make of the poor? Where and in what place of this notable sentence does he set them? He speaks not at all of them; briefly, he would have it that our charity should be first employed towards ourselves, which they have well marked and followed who say that a well ordered charity begins with himself. But this is far from the doctrine which Saint Paul teaches the Christians when he says that charity seeks not her own; and also that which Christ himself commands, to love our neighbor as ourselves. Secondly Plato places our love towards our country, thirdly our love towards our parents, and lastly our friends. And what becomes of the poor? Let them do as they can, for Plato's charity stretches not to them

~

Bacon, Speech on taking his seat in Chancery:

I will promise regularly to pronounce my decree within few days after my hearing and to sign my decree at the least in the vacation after the pronouncing, for fresh justice is the sweetest, and to the end that there be no delay of justice, nor any other means-making or laboring, but the labour of the counsel at the bar

Anti-Machiavel:

And as we see that the greed of wicked magistrates is cause of the length of law cases, because they desire that the parties who plead before them should serve their turn as a cow for milk, it follows that the poor people are pillaged and eaten to the bones by those horseleeches. Also contrary, when the magistrate hates greed, he will dispatch and hasten justice to parties, and not hold them long in law, neither pillage and spoil them; a thing bringing great comfort and help to the people

~

Bacon, "Of Counsel":

The wisest princes need not think it any diminution to their greatness, or derogation to their sufficiency, to rely upon counsel. God himself is not without, but hath made it one of the great names of his blessed Son; The Counsellor. Salomon hath pronounced that "in counsel is stability"

Anti-Machiavel:

For a prince, however prudent he is, ought not so much to esteem his own wisdom as to despise the counsel of other wise men. Solomon despised them not, and Charles the Wise always conferred of his affairs with the wise men of his council

~

Bacon, *Advancement of Learning*:

But this appeareth more manifestly, when kings themselves, or persons of authority under them, or other governors in commonwealths and popular estates, are endued with learning. For although he might be though partial to his own profession, that said "then should people and estates be happy, when either kings were philosophers, or philosophers kings"; yet so much is verified by experience, that under learned princes and governors there have ever been the best times

Anti-Machiavel:

I am content to presuppose that it is certain that there cannot come a better and more profitable thing to a people than to have a prince wise of himself; therefore, said Plato, men may call it a happy commonwealth when either the prince can play the philosopher, or when a philosopher comes to reign there

~

Bacon, *Advancement of Learning*:

For howsoever it hath been ordinary with politic men to extenuate and disable learned men by the names of *Pedantes*; yet in the records of time it appeareth in many particulars, that the governments of princes in minority (notwithstanding the infinite disadvantage of that kind of state) have nevertheless excelled the government of princes of mature age, even for that reason which they seek to traduce, which is, that by that occasion the state hath been in the hands of *Pedantes*. For so was the state of Rome for the first five years, which are so much magnified, during the minority of Nero, in the hands of Seneca, a *Pedanti*: so it was again for ten years space or more, during the minority of Gordianus the younger, with great applause and contentation in the hands of Misitheus, a *Pedanti*: so was it before that, in the minority of Alexander Severus, in like happiness, in hands not much unlike, by reason of the rule of the women, who were aided by the teachers and preceptor

Anti-Machiavel:

This may yet be better showed by the examples of many princes who have been of small wisdom and virtue, and yet notwithstanding have ruled the commonwealth well by the good and wise counsel of prudent and loyal counsellors wherewith they were served; as did the emperor Gordian the Young, who was created emperor at eleven years of age. Many judged the empire to be fallen into a childish kingdom, and so into a weakness and a bad conduction; but it proved otherwise, for this young emperor Gordian espoused the daughter of a wise man called Misitheus, whom he made the high steward of his household, and governed himself by his counsel in all his affairs; so that the Roman Empire was well ruled so long as Misitheus lived… I will not here repeat the example of the emperor Alexander Severus, who came to the empire very young, and under whom the affairs of the commonwealth were so well governed, by the means of good counsellors, as above said

~

Bacon, *Advancement of Learning*:

the writing of speculative men of active matter for the most part doth seem to men of experience, as Phormio's argument of the wars seemed to Hannibal, to be but dreams and dotage

Anti-Machiavel:

Herein it falls out to Machiavelli as it did once to the philosopher Phormio; who one day reading in the Peripatetic school of Greece, and seeing arrive and enter there Hannibal of Carthage (who was brought thither by some of his friends, to hear the eloquence of the philosopher), he began to speak and dispute with much babbling of the laws of war and the duty of a good captain, before this most famous captain, who had forgotten more than ever that proud philosopher knew or had learned. When he had thus ended his lecture and goodly disputation, as Hannibal went from the auditory one of his friends who had brought him there asked what he thought of the philosopher's eloquence and gallant speech. He said, "Truly I have seen in my life many old dotards, but I never saw one so great as this Phormio"

~

Bacon, *Advancement of Learning*:

For Machiavel noteth wisely, how Fabius Maximus would have been temporizing still, according to his old bias, when the nature of war was altered and required hot pursuit

Bacon, *Apophthegms New and Old*:

Fabius Maximus being resolved to draw the war in length, still waited upon Hannibal's progress, to curb him; and for that purpose, he encamped upon the high grounds. But Terentius his colleague fought with Hannibal, and was in great peril of overthrow. But then Fabius came down the high grounds, and got the day. Whereupon Hannibal said, That he did ever think, that that same cloud that hanged upon the hills, would at one time or other, give a tempest

Anti-Machiavel:

Seeing this, the Roman Senate sent against Hannibal Fabius Maximus, who was not so forward (and it may be not so hardy) as Flaminius or Sempronius were; but he was more wise and careful, as he showed himself. On his arrival he did not set upon Hannibal, who desired no other thing, but began to coast him far off, seeking always advantageous places. And when Hannibal approached him, then would he show him a countenance fully determined to fight, yet always seeking places of advantage. But Hannibal, who was not so rash as to join with his enemy to his own disadvantage, made a show to recoil and fly, to draw him after him. Fabius followed him, but upon coasts and hills, seeking always not the shortest way, but that way which was most for his advantage. Hannibal saw him always upon some hill or coast near him, as it were a cloud over his head; so that after Hannibal had many times essayed to draw Fabius into a place fit for himself, and where he might give battle for his own good, and yet could not thereunto draw him, said: "I see well now that the Romans also have gotten a Hannibal; and I fear that this cloud, which approaching us, still hovers upon those hills, will one of these mornings pour out some shower on our heads"

~

Bacon, "Of the True Greatness of Kingdoms and Estates":

A civil war, indeed, is like the heat of a fever; but a foreign war is like the heat of exercise, and serveth to keep the body in health

Anti-Machiavel:

Therefore a foreign war seems not to be very damaging, but something necessary to occupy and exercise his subjects; but domestic and civil wars must be shunned and extinguished with all our power, for they are things against the right of nature, to make war against the people of their own country, as he that does it against his own entrails

~

Bacon, "Of Unity in Religion":

But we may not take up the third sword, which is Mahomet's sword, or like unto it; that is, to propagate religion by wars or by sanguinary persecutions to force consciences

Bacon, "Advertisement Touching a Holy War":

I was ever of opinion, that the Philosopher's Stone, and a Holy War, were but the *rendez-vous* of cracked brains

Anti-Machiavel:

But here may arise a question, if it is lawful for a prince to make war for religion, and to constrain men to be of his religion. Hereupon to take the thing by reason, the resolution is very easy; for seeing that all religion consists in an approbation of certain points that concern the service of God, it is certain that such an approbation depends upon the persuasion which is given to men thereof. But the means to persuade a thing to any man is not to take weapons to beat him, nor to menace him, but to demonstrate to him by good reasons and allegations what may induce him to a persuasion.

∼

Bacon, "Of the Vicissitude of Things":

Surely there is no better way to stop the rising of new sects and schisms, than to reform abuses; to compound the smaller differences; to proceed mildly, and not with sanguinary persecutions; and rather to take the principal authors by winning and advancing them, than to enrage them by violence and bitterness

Anti-Machiavel:

It is then very much expedient, if a man means to gather fruit, and do good by his speech, to use gentle and civil talk and persuasions, especially if he has to do with a prince or great man, who will not be gained by rigor (or as they say, by high wrestling), but by mild and humble persuasions

∼

Anti-Machiavel:

For that cynical liberty of some philosophers, who knew not how to reprehend and show men's faults but by taunts and bitter biting speeches, are not to be approved; as did that fool Diogenes, who ridiculously and triflingly talked with king Alexander the Great as if he had spoken to some simple burgher of Athens. And Callisthenes, whom Alexander led with him in his voyage into Asia, to instruct him in good documents of wisdom; who indeed was so austere, hard, and biting in all his remonstrances and reasonings, that neither the king nor any others could take in good part anything he taught

Bacon, "A Proposal for Amending the Laws of England":

Callisthenes, that followed Alexander's court, and was grown in some displeasure with him, because he could not well brook the Persian adoration; at a supper, which with the Grecians was ever a great part talk, was desired, because he was an eloquent man, to speak of some theme; which he did, and chose for his theme the praise of the Macedonian nation; which though it were but a filling thing to praise men to their faces, yet he did it with such advantage of truth, and avoidance of flattery, and with such life, as the hearers were so ravished with it that they plucked the roses off from their garlands, and threw them upon him; as the manner of applause then was. Alexander was not pleased with it, and by way of discountenance said, It was easy to be a good orator in a pleasing theme: "But," saith he to Callisthenes, "turn your stile, and tell us now of our faults, that we may have the profit, and not you only the praise"; which he presently did with such a force, and so piquantly, that Alexander said, The goodness of this theme had made him eloquent before; but now it was the malice of his heart, that had inspired him

~

Anti-Machiavel:

When Alexander the Great departed from Macedonia to go to the conquest of Asia, he had all the captains of his army appear before him, and distributed to them almost all the revenue of his kingdom, leaving himself almost nothing. One of the captains, named Perdicas, said to him: "What then will you keep for yourself?" "Even hope," answered Alexander

Bacon, *Advancement of Learning*:

Lastly, weigh that quick and acute reply which he made when he gave so large gifts to his friends and servants, and was asked what he did reserve for himself, and he answered, "Hope"

~

Anti-Machiavel:

Hereof we read a very remarkable example above others in Alexander the Great, king of Macedon. When he departed from his country to pass into Asia, to make war upon that great dominator Darius, he had with him first in his love among others, Craterus and Hephaestion, two gentlemen, his best friends and servants. Yet they were far different from each other, for Craterus was of a hard and sharp wit, severe, stoic, and melancholic, who altogether gave himself unto affairs of counsel, and indeed was one of the king's chief counsellors. But Hephaestion was a young gentleman, well complexioned and conditioned in his manners and behavior, of a good and quick wit, yet free of all care but to content and please the king in his sports and pastimes. They called Craterus the king's friend, and Hephaestion the friend of Alexander, as one that gave himself to maintain the person of his prince in mirths and pastimes, which were good for the maintenance of his health

Bacon, *Advancement of Learning*:

For matter of policy, weigh that significant division, so much in all ages embraced, that he made between his two friends Hephaestion and Craterus, when he said, "that the one loved Alexander, and the other loved the king"; describing the principal difference of princes' best servants, that some in affection love their person, and others in duty love their crown

∼

Bacon, "A Proposal for Amending the Laws of England":

For the laws of Lycurgus, Solon, Minos, and others of ancient time, they are not the worse because grammar scholars speak of them

Anti-Machiavel:

So is there great need of some Lycurgus or Solon to make those laws, men's wits are so wild, and their spirits so marvelously plentiful and fertile to bring forth contentions and differences, and so easily to dissent from each other

∼

Bacon, "Of Anger":

Anger is a kind of baseness, as it appears well in the weakness of whose subjects in whom it reigns

Anti-Machiavel:

This vice of cruelty, proceeding from the weakness of those who cannot command their choler and passions of vengeance, and suffer themselves to be governed by them, never happened in a generous and valiant heart, but rather always in cowardly and fearful hearts

Bacon, "Of Revenge":

Revenge is a kind of wild justice, which the more a man's nature runs to, the more ought law to weed it out

Anti-Machiavel:

And if it were lawful for everyone to use vengeance, that would be to introduce a confusion and disorder into the commonwealth, and to enterprise upon the right which belongs to the magistrate, unto whom God has given the sword, to do right to everyone and to punish those who are faulty, according to their merits

Bacon, "Of Revenge":

Public revenges are for the most part fortunate; as that for the death of Caesar; for the death of Pertinax; for the death of Henry the Third of France; and many more

Anti-Machiavel:

Moreover, he exercised part of his cruelties in the revenge of the good emperor Pertinax, which was a lawful cause; yet withal he had in himself many goodly and laudable virtues, as we have in other places rehearsed

Bacon, *History of the Reign of King Henry VII*:

After that Richard, the third of that name, king in fact only, but tyrant both in title and regiment, and so commonly termed and reputed in all times since, was by the Divine Revenge, favouring the design of an exiled man, overthrown and slain at Bosworth Field; there succeeded in the kingdom the Earl of Richmond, thenceforth styled Henry the Seventh

Anti-Machiavel:

A similar punishment happened by the judgment of God to that cruel king Richard of England, brother of Edward IV… Yet that king, who despaired otherwise to be maintained in his estate, gave battle to the earl and was slain fighting, after he had reigned about a year. And the earl of Richmond went right to London with his victory, and the slaying of that tyrant; then he took out of the monastery Edward's two daughters, espoused the elder, and was straight made king of England, called Henry VII, grandfather of the most illustrious queen Elizabeth presently reigning

~

Bacon, "Of Friendship":

The like or more was between Septimus Severus and Plautianus. For he forced his eldest son to marry the daughter of Plautianus; and would often maintain Plautianus in doing affronts to his son; and did write also in a letter to the senate, by these words: "I love the man so well, as I wish he may over-live me"

Anti-Machiavel:

The emperor Severus advanced Plautianus so high, that being great master of his household, the people thought he was the emperor himself, and that Severus was but his great master

~

Bacon, "Of Friendship":

Augustus raised Agrippa (though of mean birth) to that height, as when he consulted with Maecenas about the marriage of his daughter Julia, Maecenas took the liberty to tell him, that "he must either marry his daughter to Agrippa, or take away his life: there was no third way, he had made him so great"

Anti-Machiavel:

And here that manner of electing friends which Augustus Caesar observed is worthy of observation. For he did not easily retain every man in his friendship and familiarity, but took time to prove and find their virtues, fidelity, and loyalty. Those he knew to be virtuous people, and who would freely tell him the truth of all things (as did that good and wise Maecenas), and who would not flatter him, but would employ good will sincerely in the charges he gave them—after he had well proved them, then would he acknowledge them his friends

Bacon, *De augmentis scientiarum*:

When the prince is one who lends an easy and credulous ear without discernment to whisperers and informers, there breathes as it were from the king himself a pestilent air, which corrupts and infects all his servants. Some probe the fears and jealousies of the prince, and increase them with false tales

Anti-Machiavel:

A marmoset, according to the language of our elders, is as much to say a reporter, murmurer, whisperer of tales behind one's back in princes' and great men's ears, which are false, or else not to be reiterated or reported

~

Bacon, "Of the True Greatness of Kingdoms and Estates":

And, certainly those degenerate arts and shifts, whereby many counsellors and governors gain both favour with their masters and estimation with the vulgar, deserve no better name than fiddling; being things rather pleasing for the time, and graceful to themselves only, than tending to the weal and advancement of the state which they serve

Anti-Machiavel:

First, there are those our ancient Frenchmen called janglers, which signifies as much as a scoffer, a trifler, a man full of words, or as we call them, long tongues, who by their jangling and babbling in rhyme or in prose give themselves to please great men, in praising and exalting them exceedingly, and rather for their vices than for their virtues

~

Bacon, "Of Friendship":

So as there is as much difference between the counsel that a friend giveth, and that a man giveth himself, as there is between the counsel of a friend and of a flatterer; for there is no such flatterer as is a man's self, and there is no such remedy against flattery of a man's self as the liberty of a friend

Anti-Machiavel:

And above all, men ought well to engrave in princes' minds that notable answer that Phocion made unto the king Antipater, who had required something of him which was not reasonable. "I would, sir, do for you service all that is possible for me, but you cannot have me both for a friend and a flatterer." As if he would say that they be two things far different, to be a friend and to be a flatterer, as in truth they are

~

Bacon, *Ornamenta Rationalia*:

The coward calls himself a cautious man; and the miser says, he is frugal

Anti-Machiavel:

And it helps to this persuasion that the flatterer always takes for the subject of his praises those vices which are in alliance and neighborhood with their virtues. For if the prince is cruel and violent, he will persuade him that he is magnanimous and generous, and such a one as will not put up with an injury. If the prince is prodigal, he will make him believe that he is liberal and magnificent, that he maintains an estate truly royal, and one that well recompenses his servants. If the prince is overgone in lubricities and lusts, he will say he is of a humane and manly nature, of a jovial and merry complexion, and of no saturnine complexion or condition. If the prince is covetous and an eater of his subjects, he will say he is worthy to be a great prince as he is, because he knows well how to make himself well obeyed. Briefly, the flatterer adorns his language in such sort that he will always praise the prince's vice by the resemblance of some virtue near thereunto. For most vices have a likeness with some virtue

~

Bacon, *Ornamenta Rationalia*:

He that injures one, threatens an hundred… he of whom many are afraid, ought himself to fear many

Anti-Machiavel:

Moreover, cruelty is always hated by everyone; for although it be not practiced upon all individuals, but upon some only, yet those upon whom it is not exercised cease not to fear when they see it executed upon their parents, friends, allies, and neighbors. But the fear of pain and punishment engenders hatred; for one can never love that whereof he fears to receive evil, and especially when there is a fear of life, loss of goods, and honors, which are the things we hold most precious

∼

Bacon, *Ornamenta Rationalia*:

He conquers twice, who restrains himself in victory

Anti-Machiavel:

The clemency of a prince is the cause of the increase of his domination. Hereupon we read a memorable history of Romulus, who was so clement, soft, and gentle towards the people he vanquished and subjugated, that not only many individuals but the whole multitude of people submitted themselves voluntarily and unconstrainedly under his obedience. The same virtue was also the cause that Julius Caesar vanquished the Gauls; for he was so soft and gracious to them, and so easy to pardon, and used them every way so well, far from oppression, that many of that nation voluntarily joined themselves unto him, and by them he vanquished the others. When Alexander the Great made great conquests in Asia, most commonly the citizens of all great cities met him to present him with the keys of the towns; for he dealt with them in such clemency and kindness, without in any way altering their estates, that they liked better to be his than their own

∼

Bacon, *Advancement of Learning*:

When Periander, being consulted how to preserve a tyranny newly usurped, bid the messenger report what he saw; and going into the garden, cropped all the tallest flowers; he thus used as strong an hieroglyphic as if he had drawn it upon paper

Anti-Machiavel:

Periander, having tyrannously obtained the crown of Corinth where he had no right, fearing some conspiracy against him, sent a messenger to ask advice of his great friend Thrasibulus, so to be assured master and lord of Corinth. Thrasibulus made him no answer by mouth; but commanding the messenger to follow him, he went into a field full of ripe corn, and taking the highest and most eminent ears there, he bruised them between his hands and wished the messenger to return to Periander, saying no more unto him. As soon as Periander heard of bruising the most ancient ears of corn, he presently conceived the meaning thereof; to wit, to overthrow and remove all the great men of Corinth who suffered any loss and were grieved at the change of the state; as indeed he did

~

Bacon, *Advancement of Learning*:

And the virtue of this prince, continued with that of his predecessor, made the name of Antoninus so sacred in the world, that though it were extremely dishonoured in Commodus, Caracalla, and Heliogabalus, who all bare the name, yet when Alexander Severus refused the name because he was a stranger to the family, the Senate with one acclamation said, *Quomodo Augustus, sic et Antoninus*: in such renown and veneration was the name of these two princes in those days, that they would have had it as a perpetual addition in all the emperors' style

Anti-Machiavel:

The very name of Antoninus was also so reverenced and loved by all the world, from father to son in generations after him many successive emperors caused themselves to be called Antonys, that rather they might be beloved of the people, though that name did not belong to them, nor were of the race or family of Antoninus; as did Diodumenus, Macrinus his son and companion in the empire, and as also did Bassianus and Geta, Severus' children, and Heliogabalus, they were all surnamed Antoninus. But as this name appertained not to them, so they held nothing of the virtues of that good emperor, with whose name they decked themselves

Antony & Cleopatra:

> Sir, sometimes when he is not Antony
> He comes too short of that great property
> Which still should go with Antony

~

Bacon, "Charge against Somerset":

So it appeareth likewise in Scripture, that the murder of Abner by Joab, though it were by David respited in respect of great services past, or reason of state, yet it was not forgotten

Anti-Machiavel:

For the last example of this matter, I will set down that of Joab, David's nephew and constable, unto whom he did great services. Yet David commanded his son Solomon that he should put to death his cousin Joab, because of his perfidy

~

Bacon, *Advancement of Learning*:

So likewise in the person of Solomon the king, we see the gift or endowment of wisdom and learning, both in Solomon's petition and in God's assent thereunto, preferred before all other terrene and temporal felicity. By virtue of which grant or donative of God Solomon became enabled not only to write those excellent parables or aphorisms concerning divine and moral philosophy, but also to compile a natural history of all verdure, from the cedar upon the mountain to the moss upon the wall (which is but a rudiment between putrefaction and an herb), and also of all things that breathe or move. Nay, the same Solomon the king, although he excelled in the glory of treasure and magnificent buildings, of shipping and navigation, of service and attendance, of fame and renown, and the like, yet he maketh no claim to any of those glories, but only to the glory of inquisition of truth; for so he saith expressly, "The glory of God is to conceal a thing, but the glory of the king is to find it out"; as if, according to the innocent play of children, the Divine Majesty took delight to hide His works, to the end to have them found out; and as if kings could not obtain a greater honour than to be God's playfellows in that game; considering the great commandment of wits and means, whereby nothing needeth to be hidden from them

Anti-Machiavel:

Solomon was a king most wise, and a great philosopher; for he asked wisdom from God, who gave it in such abundance that besides being ignorant of nothing a prince should know to govern his subjects well, he also knew the natures of plants and living creatures, and was so cunning in all kinds of philosophy that his knowledge was admired through all the world. His prudence and wisdom made him so respected by all the great kings, his neighbors, that they esteemed themselves happy to do him pleasure and have his amity. By this means he maintained his kingdom in so high and happy a peace that in his time his subjects made no more account of silver than of stones, they had such store. And as for himself, he held so magnificent an estate, that we read not of any king or emperor that did the like

~

Bacon, *Advancement of Learning*:

Dramatic poesy, which has the theatre for its world, would be of excellent use if well directed. For the stage is capable of no small influence both of discipline and of corruption. Now of corruptions in this kind we have enough; but the discipline has in our times been plainly neglected. And though in modern states play-acting is esteemed but as a toy, except when it is too satirical and biting; yet among the ancients it was used as a means of educating men's minds to virtue

Anti-Machiavel:

After Solon had seen Thespis' first edition and action of a tragedy, and meeting with him before the play, he asked if he was not ashamed to publish such feigned fables under so noble, yet a counterfeit personage. Thespis answered that it was no disgrace upon a stage, merrily and in sport, to say and do anything. Then Solon, striking hard upon the earth with his staff, replied thus: "Yea but shortly, we that now like and embrace this play, shall find it practiced in our contracts and common affairs." This man of deep understanding saw that public discipline and reformation of manners, attempted once in sport and jest, would soon quail; and corruption, at the beginning passing in play, would fall and end in earnest

~

Bacon, *Advancement of Learning*:

So again we find that many of the ancient bishops and fathers of the Church were excellently read and studied in all the learning of the heathen... it was the Christian Church, which amidst the inundations of the Scythians on the one side from the north-west, and the Saracens from the east, did preserve in the sacred lap and bosom thereof the precious relics even of heathen learning, which otherwise had been extinguished as if no such thing had ever been

Anti-Machiavel:

But now I am desirous to know of this atheist Machiavelli, what was the cause that so many good books of the pagan authors were lost since the time of the ancient doctors of our Christian religion? Was it not by the Goths, who were pagans? For at their so many interruptions and breaking out of their countries, upon Gaul, Italy, and Spain, they wasted and burned as many books as they could find, being enemies of all learning and letters. And who within this hundred years has restored good letters contained in the books of the ancient pagans, Greeks, and Latins? Has it been the Turk, who is a pagan? It is well enough known that he is an enemy of letters, and desires none. Nay contrary, it has been the Christians who have restored them, and established them in the brightness and light wherein we see them today

~

Bacon, "Of the Colours of Good and Evil":

So the Epicures say of the Stoics' felicity placed in virtue; that it is like the felicity of a player, who if he were left of his auditory and their applause, he would straight be out of heart and countenance; and therefore they call virtue *bonum theatrale* [public good]

Anti-Machiavel:

Briefly, a man may see within man an admirable and well ordained disposition of all the parts, and it brings us necessarily (whether we will or no) to acknowledge that there must be a God, a sovereign architect, who has made this excellent building; and by these considerations of natural things, whereof I do but lightly touch the points, the ancient philosophers, as the Platonists, Aristotelians, Stoics, and others, have been brought to the knowledge of a God and of his providence. And of all the sects of philosophers, there never was any which agreed not hereunto, unless the sect of the Epicureans, who were gluttons, drunkards, and whoremongers; who constituted their sovereign felicity in carnal pleasures, wherein they wallowed like brute beasts

~

Bacon, "Of Custom and Education":

And therefore, as Machiavel well noteth, though in an ill-favoured instance, there is no trusting to the force of nature, nor to the bravery of words, except it be corroborate by custom. His instance is, that for the achieving of a desperate conspiracy, a man should not rest upon the fierceness of any man's nature, or his resolute undertakings, but take such a one as both had his hands formerly in blood

Anti-Machiavel:

Catiline, a man devoid of all virtue and a bundle of all vice, resolving in his brain to be an exceedingly great man or altogether nothing, devised a conspiracy against his country and drew to his league many Roman gentlemen such as himself. Considering that he could not bring to effect his conjuration without declaring and communicating it to the chieftains of his aid, yet fearing that some of them would disclose it, he made them all take a most execrable oath, that thereby might be foreclosed from them all hope of retiring from his side. So he mixed wine with human blood in pots and made all his companions drink of it, and made them swear with an execration that they would never disclose the enterprise, but employ themselves with all their power to execute it. His partners, already culpable of human blood, were so secret that nothing would have been discovered if God had not permitted a harlot called Fulvia to draw certain words out of a conspirator's mouth, as she demanded of him where he lay the preceding nights. Being drunk, to enjoy his courtesan he disclosed to her that he had been in a company with whom he made an enterprise that would make him rich forever. As soon as Fulvia knew all the conjuration she disclosed it to the consul Cicero. Cicero did what he could to open all the enterprise, but the conspirators held so well their horrible oath that not one of so great a number would ever reveal a word. But yet Cicero found means to know all, by the declaration which the Allobroges made, who Catiline had appointed to furnish him with people for the execution. But the end of Catiline was such that he was slain fighting with a great number of others, and most of his accomplices were executed by justice. Briefly, all who have practiced that wicked doctrine of Machiavelli, to commit outrageous acts to be irreconcilable, their ends and lives have proved very tragedies

~

Bacon, "Of the Colours of Good and Evil":

The ill that a man brings on himself by his own fault is greater; that which is brought on him from without is less. The reason is because the sting and remorse of the mind accusing itself, doubleth all adversity... So the poets in tragedies do make the most passionate lamentations, questioning, and torturing of a man's self... where the evil is derived from a man's own fault, there all strikes deadly inwards, and suffocateth

Anti-Machiavel:

Men may see how an evil conscience leaves a man never in quiet. This wicked man, knowing that by his cruelty he had procured the hatred of his subjects, the wrath of God, and the enmity of all the world, was tormented in his conscience as of an infernal fury, which ever after fretted his languishing soul in the poor infected and wasted body

~

Bacon, "Notes on the Present State of Christendom":

The division in his country [France] for matters of religion and state, through miscontentment of the nobility to see strangers advanced to the greatest charges of the realm, the offices of justice sold, the treasury wasted, the people polled, the country destroyed, hath bred great trouble, and like to see more

Anti-Machiavel:

Besides the examples we read in histories, we know it by experience, seeing at this day all France fashioned after the manners, conditions, and vices of foreigners that govern it, and who have the principal charges and estates

~

Advancement of Learning:

And as Alexander Borgia was wont to say, of the expedition of the French for Naples, that they came with chalk in their hands to mark up their lodgings not with weapons to fight; so we like better, that entry of truth, which comes peaceably where the Minds of men, capable to lodge so great a guest, are signed, as it were, with chalk; than that which comes with Pugnacity, and forceth itself a way by contentions and controversies

Anti-Machiavel:

King Charles VIII, in the voyage of Naples, which he made in his own person, conquered the realm of Naples almost without striking a stroke; and was received by all the people, and most of the nobility, as a messiah sent from God to deliver them from the cruel and barbarous tyranny wherein they had long endured under their kings, Alfonso and Ferdinand of Aragon, usurpers of that kingdom from the house of Anjou, to which Charles succeeded

~

Bacon, *Novum Organum*:

We cannot command nature except by obeying her

Anti-Machiavel:

It is evident enough that the felicity of a state lies wholly in well commanding and well obeying, whereupon results a harmony and concordance so melodious and excellent, that he who commands and he who obeys both receive contentment, pleasure, and utility. But to obey well depends wholly on well commanding, and cannot be without it; so commanding well depends on the prudence and wisdom of him that commands

~

Anti-Machiavel:

And we see but too much by experience that the old proverb is true, honors change manners. You may see how the most gracious and courteous in the world, the most affable and officious to everyone (that is possible) while they are in base degree, after they are mounted into some high degree of honor and dignity they become rough and haughty, so much that those to whom they showed themselves facile and serviceable, they now seem not to know them, who before were their private friends and familiars. Such people have no good souls, but deserve that their fierceness and pride should dispossess them of that place unto which most commonly their dissembled humility and courtesy has advanced them. This vice is reprehensible, not only in a prince's officers but also in the prince himself, who ought not to put pride and fierceness upon that head whereupon the crown and diadem stands. For this the king Agamemnon is taxed and reprehended by Menelaus his brother, in a tragedy of Euripides, where he says thus:

> Most humble was thou in times past, and kissed each man's hand,
> Most humane, gentle, affable, to none thy gates did stand
> Shut up, to highest honor thou by such means sought to rise:
> But now thou honor has supreme, why proves thou so unwise,
> Another man straight to become, and change thy manners all?
> Yea human duty even to friends, by thee doth not befall.
> To good men that esteem good fame, this is not covenable,
> Chameleon like thy manners changed, thou to be so mutable.

Julius Caesar.

> He would be crowned.
> How that might change his nature, there's the question.
> It is the bright day that brings forth the adder,
> And that craves wary walking. Crown him that,
> And then I grant we put a sting in him
> That at his will he may do danger with.
> Th' abuse of greatness is when it disjoins
> Remorse from power. And to speak truth of Caesar,
> I have not known when his affections swayed
> More than his reason. But 'tis a common proof
> That lowliness is young ambition's ladder,
> Whereto the climber-upward turns his face;
> But when he once attains the upmost round
> He then unto the ladder turns his back,
> Looks in the clouds, scorning the base degrees
> By which he did ascend. So Caesar may.

A philosophi-
call discourse,

Entituled,

The Anato-
mie of the
minde.

*Nevvlie made and set forth
by T. R.*

Imprinted at
London by I. C. for Andrew
Maunsell, dvvelling in
Paules Church yarde,
at the signe of the
Parret. 1576.

2. *The Anatomie of the Minde*

The Anatomie of the Minde is a small book of essays on Greek and Roman philosophy published in 1576, the year Bacon left Cambridge. It has extensive parallels with *Anti-Machiavel*, also 1576, which is somewhat strange, as the one was published in French at Geneva and the other in English at London. The book is divided into two sections, "Perturbations" and "Moral Virtues"; each chapter bears a title like Bacon's essays, "Of Ambition," "Of Constancy," etc. The front matter includes a dedication to Sir Christopher Hatton, several poems in English and Latin, and a preface. The author describes the book as "my first fruits of study" and states

> I did once for my profit in the University draw into Latin tables, which since for thy profit (Christian Reader) at the request of a gentleman of good credit and worship, I have Englished, and published in these two books… hereafter (if God so please, and grant me life and leisure) it may be published both in sweeter phrase to delight, and in better method to profit

Several interesting things are found here; the dedication states "Virtue though in the mind of basest for condition, is very commendable. But nothing doth so set out the Diamond, as doth the Gold … virtue is then most wondered at, when it is in him which for authority is of power." Bacon's essay "Of Beauty" begins "Virtue is like a rich stone, best plain set"; Shakespeare's *Richard III*:

> A base, foul stone, made precious by the foil
> Of England's chair, where he is falsely set.

The *Anatomie*'s preface states: "he which thoroughly would know himself must as well know his body, as his mind … For by the one we participate the nature of beasts, by the other of Angels." Compare with Bacon's essay "Of Atheism":

> They that deny a God destroy a man's nobility, for certainly man is of kin to the beasts by his body; and if he be not of kin to God by his spirit, he is a base and ignoble creature

The *Anatomie*'s prefatory poem "Joshua Hutten to the Book" reads:

> For first the mind before old Adam's fall,
> from Perturbations all, was perfect free;

> But after, Motions and affections all,
> and passions came, which now their dwelling be

This was how Bacon envisioned his life's work:

> Man by the Fall fell at the same time from the state of innocence and from his dominion over creation. Both of these losses, however, can even in this life be in some part repaired; the former by religion and Faith, the latter by arts and sciences

The *Anatomie* is mentioned in Gabriel Harvey's *Pierce's Supererogation* (1593): "an anatomy of the Mind, and Fortune, were respectively as behooveful and necessary, as an Anatomy of the Body." Harvey had been Francis Bacon's rhetoric tutor at Cambridge and is credited with coining several words, including idiom, conscious, jovial, extensively, notoriety, and rascality. *Pierce's Supererogation* is also noteworthy in that it references *Venus and Adonis* before it had been published, and Harvey evidently knew it was going out under the name of Shakespeare.

Several stories found in the *Anatomie* also appear in Shakespeare; *Timon of Athens*:

> Amongst all envious persons (which have been for number infinite) none hath been so much reprehended for the same, as was Timon of Athens. For he could away with none, but only with Alcibiades; and being asked of Apemantus, why envying all others he so favored him, answered, that therefore he did love and account of him because he perceived the disposition of Alcibiades to be such as he should in time be a scourge to the Athenians, and a cause of many troubles which they should come into

Julius Caesar:

> Caesar declared himself to hate and detest those which by nature were pale and sad; and therefore on a time, as he was merely jesting with many of his familiars, but especially with one of a pleasant countenance, and of constitution of body very gross, another perceiving his great familiarity, came unto him and willed him to talk not so friendly, but to take heed of him; for without doubt, he said, if he used his company and familiarity, no good would come thereof. Then Caesar smiling said that he feared not those of merry countenance, but those lowering and sad persons, meaning Brutus and Cassius; which in deed afterwards were not only the procurers, but the committers of his cruel murdering

Julius Caesar:

> *Caesar.* Let me have men about me that are fat,

> Sleek-headed men, and such as sleep o' nights.
> Yond Cassius has a lean and hungry look.
> He thinks too much. Such men are dangerous.
> *Antony.* Fear him not, Caesar, he's not dangerous.
> He is a noble Roman, and well given.
> *Caesar.* Would he were fatter! But I fear him not.

The following scene, in which Caesar's wife Calpurnia, fearing for his life, begs him to stay home ("Your wisdom is consumed in confidence. Do not go forth today") is also anticipated in the *Anatomie*:

> Caesar likewise, being over bold and contemning the words of those which wished him well, came to a most miserable end. For oftentimes he was warned and foretold of the conspiracies of his foes to bring him to death. He was counseled to see to himself, and to guard his body, lest at any time his enemies upon the sudden should set upon him, many promising their service willingly. But he contemned all their words and would none of their service, saying that he was a miserable Prince that would have a Guard about him. But his contempt hastened his end, for as it was told him afore, his death was sought and he murdered of his Senate in their house of consultation, with penknives. If he had not so trusted to his good luck, and had such a confidence that he could have withstood all the assaults of his foes, and harkened to the wholesome admonitions of his faithful friends, his days might have been prolonged, and in time he might have turned the hearts of those which then were his capital and deadly enemies

Another echo is found in *Antony and Cleopatra*:

> Since Cleopatra died
> I have lived in such dishonor that the gods
> Detest my baseness. I, that with my sword
> Quartered the world, and o'er green Neptune's back
> With ships made cities, condemn myself to lack
> The courage of a woman—less noble mind
> Than she which by her death our Caesar tells
> "I am conqueror of myself."

Anatomie of the Minde:

> the Romans and many other nations allowed and thought well of [suicide], else would not so many so desperately have bereft themselves of life; as did Brutus and Cassius after the death of Caesar; as did Antony, when he heard that Cleopatra had killed herself; for hearing the same, he brake into these words: Die Antony, what lookest thou for? Fortune hath taken her from thee, by whom thou desiredst to prolong thy days, and therefore it shall

never be said that such a captain as I have been accounted, will be stained of a woman in stoutness of minds; and therewithal gored himself upon a sword, and so most desperately forsook this world

Bacon's heraldic motto *mediocria firma* ("the middle ground is firm") finds a parallel in the *Anatomie*:

> Aristotle said, [virtue] is a choosing habit of the mind, consisting in a mean between two extremes, of which one exceeds, the other wants much; as Fortitude when it exceeds falls into rashness, when it faints into childish fearfulness; and Liberality, when it lavishes out of reason is called prodigality, when it is not extended any whit, purchases the name of covetousness

This is also similar to *Don Quixote*:

> valor is a virtue betwixt two vicious extremes, as cowardice and rashness; but it is less dangerous for him that is valiant to rise to a point of rashness than to fall or touch upon the coward. For, as it is more easy for a prodigal man to be liberal than a covetous, so it is easier for a rash man to be truly valiant than a coward to come to true valor. And, touching the onset in adventures, believe me, Signior Don Diego, it is better playing a good trump than a small; for it sounds better in the hearer's ears, "Such a knight is rash and hardy," than "Such a knight is fearful and cowardly."' 'I say, signior,' answered Don Diego, 'that all that you have said and done is levelled out by the line of reason, and I think, if the statutes and ordinances of knight-errantry were lost, they might be found again in your breast, as in their own storehouse and register

The last sentence is echoed in the *Advancement of Learning*; "certain critics are used to say, that if all sciences were lost, they might be found in Virgil." The entire passage is strongly echoed in *Wisdom of the Ancients*:

> the path of virtue lies straight between excess on the one side, and defect on the other. And no wonder that excess should prove the bane of Icarus, exulting in juvenile strength and vigor; for excess is the natural vice of youth, as defect is that of old age; and if a man must perish by either, Icarus chose the better of the two; for all defects are justly esteemed more depraved than excesses. There is some magnanimity in excess, that, like a bird, claims kindred with the heavens; but defect is a reptile, that basely crawls upon the earth

The next book we will visit, *The French Academy* states:

> [virtue] holds a man within the limits of prowess and valor, lest he should cast away himself through rashness or cowardice; she causes him wisely to use liberality, because he should not be spoiled by covetousness or fall into prodigality

In *The Mystery of Francis Bacon* William Smedley theorized that Bacon wrote both the *Anatomie* and another (unnamed) book published shortly thereafter, which may have been *Anti-Machiavel*. Smedley did not give his reasons for essaying this attribution, but only wrote the following:

> The following suggestion is put forward with all diffidence, but after long and careful investigation. Francis Bacon was the author of two books which were published, one before he left England, and the other shortly after. The first is a philosophical discourse entitled *The Anatomie of the Minde*. "Newlie made and set forth by T.R. Imprinted at London by I.C. for Andrew Maunsell," 1576, 12mo. The dedication is addressed to Master Christopher Hatton, and the name of Tho. Rogers is attached to it. There was a Thomas Rogers who was Chaplain to Archbishop Bancroft, and the book has been attributed to him, apparently only because no other of the same name was known. There was published in 1577 a translation by Rogers of a Latin book "Of the Ende of the World, etc." and there are other translations by him published between then and 1628. There are several sermons, also, but the style of these, the matter, and the manner of treatment are quite distinct from those of the book under consideration. There is nothing of his which would support the assignment to him of *The Anatomie of the Minde*. It is foreign to his style. Having regard to the acknowledged custom of the times of putting names other than the author's on title pages, there is no need for any apology for expressing doubt as to whether the book has been correctly placed to the credit of the Bishop Bancroft's chaplain . . . There is in existence a copy of the book with the printer's and other errors corrected in Bacon's own handwriting.

Parallelisms

Anatomie of the Minde:

The Poets feign Envy to be one of the furies of Hell, and to be fed with nothing but adders and snakes . . . The Poets feign Prometheus to be tied on the top of the mountain Caucasus, and an Eagle to be gnawing of his heart . . . the Poets feigned a notable example of Thamyras

Bacon, *Wisdom of the Ancients*:

The poets feign that Vulcan attempted the chastity of Minerva, and impatient of refusal, had recourse to force

Bacon, *De augmentis scientiarum*:

true history may be written in verse and feigned history in prose ... And under the name of Poesy, I treat only of feigned history

The division of Poesy which is aptest and most according to the propriety thereof, besides those divisions which it has in common with History (for there are feigned Chronicles, feigned Lives, and feigned Relations), is into Poesy Narrative, Dramatic, and Parabolical

As You Like It:

> No, truly; for the truest poetry is the most feigning,
> and lovers are given to poetry; and what they swear in poetry may
> be said as lovers they do feign

> thou swear'st to me thou art honest;
> now, if thou wert a poet, I might have some hope thou didst
> feign

Midsummer Night's Dream:

> Thou hast by moonlight at her window sung,
> With feigning voice verses of feigning love

Merchant of Venice:

> Their savage eyes turn'd to a modest gaze
> By the sweet power of music: therefore the poet
> Did feign that Orpheus drew trees, stones and floods;
> Since nought so stockish, hard and full of rage,
> But music for the time doth change his nature

French Academy II:

So that we have in that part as it were a spiritual eye, which is much more excellent and profitable, then if we had bodily eyes there, as we have before, or else a face before and another behind, as the Poets feigned that Janus had

Anti-Machiavel:

After Solon had seen Thespis' first edition and action of a tragedy, and meeting with him before the play, he asked if he was not ashamed to publish such feigned fables under so noble, yet a counterfeit personage

Don Quixote:
Your feigned histories are so much the more good and delightful, by how much they come near the truth, or the likeness of it: and the true ones are so much the better, by how much the truer.

∼

Anatomie of the Minde:

he which thoroughly would know himself must as well know his body, as his mind . . . For by the one we participate the nature of beasts, by the other of Angels

Bacon, "Of Atheism":

They that deny a God destroy a man's nobility, for certainly man is of kin to the beasts by his body; and if he be not of kin to God by his spirit, he is a base and ignoble creature

∼

Anatomie of the Minde:

And the Pythagoreans were of his opinion, for their poesy was, that the heart should not be eaten. Their meaning was that cares and sadness should not consume the heart by unquieting the mind

Bacon, "Of Friendship":

The parable of Pythagoras is dark, but true; *Cor ne edito*; Eat not the heart

∼

Anatomie of the Minde:

there is none either of nature so wild, or for behavior so wicked, but in their kind (as it is for a hound natural to smell, and for a bird to fly) are desirous to learn, and be cunning in somewhat

Anti-Machiavel:

I would gladly ask this question of him that is most ignorant, vicious and carnal, whether he will not grant virtue to be a good of the soul. There is none so impudent whose conscience would not compel him to confess the same

∼

Anatomie of the Minde:

Virtue though in the mind of basest for condition, is very commendable; but nothing doth so set out the diamond, as doth the gold

Bacon, "Of Beauty":

Virtue is like a rich stone, best plain set

∼

Anatomie of the Minde:

Cato the elder was greatly delighted with such as at the least fault would blush. And so was Diogenes the Cynic; for when talking with a young man, he perceived his face to be red with blushing, said unto him; be of good cheer my son, for this color, is the color of virtue itself

Bacon, *The Advancement of Learning*:

it was truly said, *rubor est virtutis color* [a blush is virtue's color]

1 Henry VI:

> And, which became him like a prince indeed,
> He made a blushing cital of himself,
> And chid his truant youth with such a grace
> As if he mastered there a double spirit
> Of teaching and of learning instantly

Anatomie of the Minde:

Cicero says that Constancy is the health of the mind, so that by the same he understands the whole force and efficacy of wisdom, and that appears very well by her contrary. For Foolishness is nothing but a lightness and inconstancy of mind. Wherefore this constant man cannot be too much praised, seeing that either whole wisdom, or the very force of wisdom is in nothing more apparent than in Constancy

Anti-Machiavel:

I will then presuppose that constancy is a quality which ordinarily accompanies all other virtues; it is, as it were, of their substance and nature

Bacon, *De augmentis scientiarum*:

Constancy is the foundation on which virtues rest

Measure for Measure:

It is virtuous to be constant in any undertaking

Two Gentlemen of Verona:

O Heaven, were man but constant, he were perfect

~

Anatomie of the Minde:

Homer, when he lived was of none account, every man contemned him, and none would vouchsafe to account him their countryman; but Homer being dead, was both lacked and longed for

Coriolanus:

> I shall be loved when I am lack'd

~

Anatomie of the Minde:

Caesar declared himself to hate and detest those which by nature were pale and sad; and therefore on a time, as he was merely jesting with many of his familiars, but especially with one of a pleasant countenance, and of constitution of body very gross, another perceiving his great familiarity, came unto him, and willed him to talk not so friendly, but to take heed of him; for without doubt, he said, if he used his company and familiarity, no good would come thereof. Then Caesar smiling, said that he feared not those of merry countenance, but those lowering and sad persons, meaning Brutus and Cassius; which in deed afterwards were not only the procurers, but the committers of his cruel murdering

Julius Caesar:

> *Caesar.* Let me have men about me that are fat,
> Sleek-headed men, and such as sleep o' nights.
> Yond Cassius has a lean and hungry look.
> He thinks too much. Such men are dangerous.
>
> *Antony.* Fear him not, Caesar, he's not dangerous.
> He is a noble Roman, and well given.
>
> *Caesar.* Would he were fatter! But I fear him not.
> Yet if my name were liable to fear,
> I do not know the man I should avoid
> So soon as that spare Cassius. He reads much,
> He is a great observer, and he looks
> Quite through the deeds of men. He loves no plays,
> As thou dost, Antony; he hears no music.
> Seldom he smiles, and smiles in such a sort
> As if he mocked himself and scorned his spirit
> That could be moved to smile at anything.
> Such men as he be never at heart's ease
> Whiles they behold a greater than themselves,
> And therefore are they very dangerous.
> I rather tell thee what is to be feared
> Than what I fear, for always I am Caesar.

~

Anatomie of the Minde:

the Romans and many other nations allowed and thought well of [suicide]; else would not so many so desperately have bereft themselves of life; as did Brutus and Cassius after the death of Caesar; as did Antony, when he heard that Cleopatra had killed herself. For hearing the same, he broke into these words: "Die Antony, what lookst thou for? Fortune hath taken her from thee, by whom thou desired to prolong thy days, and therefore it shall never be said that such a captain as I have been accounted will be stained of a woman in stoutness of minds"; and therewithal gored himself upon a sword, and so most desperately forsook this world

Antony and Cleopatra:

> Since Cleopatra died
> I have lived in such dishonor that the gods
> Detest my baseness. I, that with my sword
> Quartered the world, and o'er green Neptune's back
> With ships made cities, condemn myself to lack
> The courage of a woman – less noble mind
> Than she which by her death our Caesar tells
> "I am conqueror of myself"

~

Anatomie of the Minde:

Alexander the great, liberally bestowing many things upon his friends, upon a time Perdicas spoke unto him on this manner; If you thus largely still bestow your goods, O bountiful Prince, I marvel at the length, what you will keep for yourself? Then answered Alexander, for myself I reserve Hope

Anti-Machiavel:

When Alexander the Great departed from Macedonia to go to the conquest of Asia, he had all the captains of his army appear before him, and distributed to them almost all the revenue of his kingdom, leaving himself almost nothing. One of the captains, named Perdicas, said to him: "What then will you keep for yourself?" "Even hope," answered Alexander

Bacon, Advancement of Learning:

Lastly, weigh that quick and acute reply which [Alexander] made when he gave so large gifts to his friends and servants, and was asked what he did reserve for himself, and he answered, "Hope"

Anatomie of the Minde:

there is none either of nature so wild, or for behavior so wicked, but in their kind (as it is for a hound natural to smell, and for a bird to fly) are desirous to learn, and be cunning in somewhat

Anti-Machiavel:

I would gladly ask this question of him that is most ignorant, vicious and carnal, whether he will not grant virtue to be a good of the soul. There is none so impudent whose conscience would not compel him to confess the same

Anatomie of the Minde:

And therefore true is that saying of a learned man, It is hard in prosperity to know whether our friends do love us for our own sakes, or for our goods; but adversity proves a friend. For neither doth prosperity manifest a friend, nor adversity bide a flatterer

Anti-Machiavel:

The true friend perseveres in the service of his prince, as well in time of adversity as prosperity; and the flatterer turns his back in time of adversity . . . Adversity also is a true touchstone to prove who are feigned or true friends; for when a man feels labyrinths of troubles fall on him, dissembling friends depart from him, and those who are good abide with him, as said the poet Euripides:

> Adversity the best and certain'st friends doth get,
> Prosperity both good and evil alike doth fit

Anti-Machiavel:

Amity, said Cicero, is the true bond of all human society; and whoever will take amity away from among men, as Machiavelli does from among princes, he seeks to take away all pleasure, solace, contentment, and assurance that can be among humans

Anatomie of the Minde:

Which made Cicero to say that he which would cut off this common friendship did even as it were go about to take the Sun from the world

~

Anatomie of the Minde:

The love of our Country and Prince should be great. For (as Plato and Cicero do say) no man is born for himself, but a part of our birth our Country, a part our Parents, a part our friends challenge as due unto them

Anti-Machiavel:

For proof hereof I will take the maxim of Plato, that we are not only born for ourselves, but that our birth is partly for our country, partly for our parents, and partly for our friends

~

Anti-Machiavel:

as the poet Sophocles says:

> Men must not seek, nor love, of all things to get gain,
> For he that draws gain out of that which is naught,
> Before he profit gets, shall sooner loss sustain:
> For evil gotten goods are often dearly bought

Anatomie of the Minde:

Therefore we will here conclude and say with Solon, that riches ought to be gotten, but yet after honest means, not covetously, that is by wicked arts. *Male parta, male dilabuntur*, Ill gotten goods are ill spent, says Tully

~

Anti-Machiavel:

Finally, what mischiefs have there ever been in the world which that hideous monster perfidy has not engendered? Assuredly it is an Alecto, an infernal fury, excited and called lately from hell to the vexation and utter overthrow of this poor world

Anatomie of the Minde:

And Sallust very notably says that by discord the greatest things come to naught; which agrees to that fiction of the Poets, who say that by discord, which is called Alecto, one of the furies of hell, the world, and all things else shall perish

∼

Anatomie of the Minde:

Scipio . . . was commonly wont to say, he had rather save one citizen than slay a thousand enemies

Anti-Machiavel:

Here I may not forget a notable sentence of the emperor Antonius Pius, which he received from Scipio the African, which was this: That he loved better to preserve one of his subjects than to slay a thousand of his enemies

∼

Anatomie of the Minde:

It happened after that the Carthaginians being sorely foiled in battle were enforced to send Legates to Rome to entreat for peace. Hamilcar was chosen Ambassador, but calling unto mind their ill intreating of Cornelius Asina, refused to go. Then they chose Hanno, which went boldly to Rome to the Senate house, where one of the Tribunes began openly to accuse him of unfaithfulness; but the Consuls hearing thereof, commanded him to hold his peace, and said unto Hanno; Fear not, for the faithfulness of the Romans, doth rid thee from all fear of revenge; and though we have thee now in our claws, and may do with thee what we list, yet shall it not be said that treacherously we will deal with any

Bacon, *Apophthegms*:

Hanno the Carthaginian was sent commissioner by the state, after the second Carthaginian war, to Rome, to supplicate for peace, and in the end obtained it. Yet one of the sharper senators said: You have often broken with us the peaces whereunto you have been sworn; I pray, by what Gods will you swear? Hanno answered: By the same Gods that have punished the former perjury so severely

Anatomie of the Minde:

Scipio was no Philosopher by profession, but a warrior (a strange thing, that one of that sort should be so pure from unchaste cogitations), and yet being of the age of three and twenty years, and having brought under the subjection of the Romans a city in Spain, a certain Damsel without comparison among all the captives, most beautiful, was brought unto him for delectation after all his troubles. But Scipio, before he would receive any recreation at her hands, demanded what she was; which, when he understood her to be espoused unto a young man called Luceius, he thought it a shame for him to use her company beyond honesty; and so with many precious gifts and jewels, sent her safely conducted to her husband, that should be. This continence of Scipio passes all the rest. For who would think that a warrior, from a woman; a lusty young man, from a beautiful maiden; a conqueror, from a captive having time, place, and permission (so that without controlment of any man, he might have used her) would contain himself, all things falling so in the nick? And yet this noble warrior, lusty youth, and victorious conqueror, entered not familiarity with this woman, this beautiful maiden, and captive, because she had given her truth to another. O unspeakable virtue, and most wonderful continence of this noble Scipio, which so preferred honesty before lechery; chastity before incontinence; and a faithful promise, before sinful pleasure. I may not in Rhetorical manner enlarge this matter (and yet too much cannot be spoken to his praise) and therefore I leave it

Anti-Machiavel:

Yet the example of clemency in Scipio Africanus is more notable than this of his father and uncle. After the deaths of his said father and uncle, this young lord full of all generosity and hardiness came to besiege New Carthage in Spain, and got it by assault… Among other hostages, there was a young lady of a great house brought to Scipio, who was of so great beauty that as she passed by she drew each man's regard upon her. This lady was affianced to one Allucius, prince of the Celts. Scipio, taking knowledge of her parents and to whom she was affianced, and that Allucius extremely loved her, sent for them all… The said lady's parents stepped forward and presented to him a great quantity of gold and silver for their daughter's ransom, which though Scipio refused it, they pressed it so sore upon him that he accorded to take it, and bade them lay it before him. Scipio called Allucius and said to him, Good friend, besides the dowry which your father-in-law will give you, my desire is that you will take this silver at my hands as an increase of her dowry

French Academy:

Scipio Africanus, general of the Romans, at the taking of the city of Carthage had a young damsel taken prisoner, of rare and excellent beauty. And when he understood of what great calling she came, and how her parents not long before had betrothed her to a great lord of Spain, he commanded that he should be sent for, and restored her unto him without abusing her in any respect, although he was in the flower of his age and had free and sovereign authority. Moreover, he gave for a dowry with her the money that was brought unto him for her ransom

~

Anatomie of the Minde:

Fabius Verruscosus (which for his virtues was called Maximus) which by circumspection did so abate the haughty courage of that victorious Hannibal, as among his friends and companions he would say that he never knew what war meant, before he had occasion to encounter with Fabius. Afterward was by the Roman Senate sent unto Fabius Maximus, Marcellus which likewise was a terror unto Hannibal. And therefore as he acknowledged Fabius to be his master, and to teach him to guide an army, so did he confess himself to stand in fear of Marcellus. Whose wisdom and circumspection was of the Romans so well noted as one of them, Fabius was called the buckler, the other Marcellus the sword (to cut off the enemies) of the people of Rome. So that as Cepio and Flaminius, for their temerity have been odious; so Fabius and Marcellus for their circumspection have been glorious in the eyes of all men

The Advancement of Learning:

Machiavel noteth wisely, how Fabius Maximus would have been temporizing still, according to his old bias, when the nature of war was altered and required hot pursuit." Anti-Machiavel: relates that "the Roman Senate sent against Hannibal Fabius Maximus, who was not so forward (and it may be not so hardy) as Flaminius or Sempronius were; but he was more wise and careful, as he showed himself

Bacon, *Apophthegms New and Old*:

Fabius Maximus being resolved to draw the war in length, still waited upon Hannibal's progress, to curb him; and for that purpose, he encamped upon the high grounds. But Terentius his colleague fought with Hannibal, and was in great peril of overthrow. But then Fabius came down from the high grounds, and got the day. Whereupon Hannibal said, That he did ever think, that that same cloud that hanged upon the hills, would at one time or other, give a tempest

Anti-Machiavel:

On his arrival he did not set upon Hannibal, who desired no other thing, but began to coast him far off, seeking always advantageous places. And when Hannibal approached him, then would he show him a countenance fully determined to fight, yet always seeking places of advantage. But Hannibal, who was not so rash as to join with his enemy to his own disadvantage, made a show to recoil and fly, to draw him after him. Fabius followed him, but upon coasts and hills, seeking always not the shortest way, but that way which was most for his advantage. Hannibal saw him always upon some hill or coast near him, as it were a cloud over his head; so that after Hannibal had many times essayed to draw Fabius into a place fit for himself, and where he might give battle for his own good, and yet could not thereunto draw him, said: "I see well now that the Romans also have gotten a Hannibal; and I fear that this cloud, which approaching us, still hovers upon those hills, will one of these mornings pour out some shower on our heads"

~

Anatomie of the Minde:

And that Prince which according to reason, doth govern is called a King. So that the difference between him and a Tyrant, is because a King rules as he ought, a Tyrant as he list; a King to the profiting of all, a Tyrant only to pleasure a few, and that not for the love of virtue, but to the increase of wickedness

Anti-Machiavel:

As contrary, none can love tyranny but must be an enemy to the common weal. For tyranny draws all to itself and despoils subjects of their goods and commodities, to appropriate all to itself, making its particular good from what belongs to all men and applying to its own profit and use what should serve for all men in general. So it follows that whoever loves the profit of a tyrant consequently hates the profit of his subjects, and he who loves the common good of subjects hates the particular profit of a tyrant

~

Anatomie of the Minde:

Julius Caesar, though much reprehended in respect of the civil discord between him and Pompey, yet is he greatly adorned with commendations, for severe punishing the most cruel murderers of his capital enemy Pompey

Anti-Machiavel:

In like manner was the subtle disputation of those who caused the famous captain Pompey to die. After he lost the battle of Pharsalia against Caesar, he embarked on the sea with his wife and friends, hovering about Egypt, hoping to be entertained by the young king Ptolemy in consideration of the pleasures he had done to his father. At his approach he sent a messenger to know if Ptolemy would receive him in assurance; but the king's affairs were then managed by three base persons who understood nothing less than how to govern affairs of state. They were Theodotus the rhetorician, his schoolmaster; Achillas, his domestic servant, and a chamberlain. These three venerable persons fell to counsel, to deliberate what answer the king should make to Pompey. At the beginning they differed in opinion, one saying it was good to receive him, the other not. But in the end all three accorded in the worst opinion they could have taken, which was to receive Pompey and slay him; which opinion this goodly rhetorician Theodotus persuaded to the other two by his subtle reasons. He said, "If we receive Pompey, it is certain we will have Caesar for an enemy and Pompey for a master. If we do not receive him, they will both be our enemies, Pompey for rejecting him and Caesar because we have not stayed him. But if we receive him and put him to death, Caesar will thank us and Pompey cannot revenge himself upon us; for a dead man is no warrior." Upon these goodly reasons of that subtle rhetorician, the conclusion was taken by these three bad people to put to death this great person Pompey, who had had so many triumphs and victories in his life, and who had sometimes seen five or six great kings wait on him at once, as an arbiter of their contentions and differences. If these bad counselors had considered the greatness of Pompey, who had so many virtuous and great lords as parents and friends, as also the magnanimity of Caesar, who would vanquish by true force and not by perfidies and treasons, they would never have stayed upon the cold and foolish subtleties of this gentle rhetorician, and they would not have concluded the death of so great a man. But yet they concluded it and executed their conclusion, putting Pompey to death as soon as he had taken port in Egypt. But it was not long before they received the reward of their perfidy; for Caesar soon arrived, unto whom Pothinus and Achillas presented the head of Pompey, thinking to please him greatly. Caesar turned his face away and began to weep, and commanded Pothinus and Achillas put to death. And that subtle reason of Theodotus, who persuaded them that Caesar would thank them for their murder, was not found true. Seeing this execution and finding himself very culpable, Theodotus fled and lived some years miserably wandering and begging here and there, fearing to be known by the world which everywhere had him in execration. But in the end, after the death of Caesar, Brutus found him by chance and caused him to die miserably, after he had made him endure infinite torments. Behold the end of those three counsellors of that young king Ptolemy, who also by their evil conducting made a poor end; for he was slain in a battle near the Nile, and none could ever find his body

~

Anatomie of the Minde:

the cause of Galba the Emperor's destruction was because he lacked this Magnanimity, and suffered himself to be governed according to the minds of three wicked men, in whose company he did much delight, which brought shame to him and confusion to his people

Anti-Machiavel:

The emperor Galba was a good and wise prince, but he suffered himself to be so governed and mastered by Titus Junius, Cornelius Lacus, and Icellus Martianus, who were of accord to rob and do evil, and brought upon Galba a common report to be a wicked and unworthy emperor. For his dealings and dispositions were not of one same tenor and constancy as they ought to have been; sometimes he showed himself too sparing, sometimes too prodigal; now remiss and negligent, now too near a taker; often he would refuse things which were not to be refused, or grant that which ought not to have been granted. He condemned noble persons upon simple suspicions; yet he would never accord to the Roman people to punish Tigellinus and Halotus, the ministers of Nero culpable of great wickedness, but contrarily favored them, and advanced Halotus into a high estate. He suffered these three counsellors and governors to sell and give tributes, freedoms, pardons for faults, and all other things. By such means Galba got the evil will of all estates, noblemen, senators, magistrates, and common people; insomuch that he was slain after reigning but seven months. And he received this end because he let himself be mastered by three alone; whereas if he had had a good council, composed of a good number of good and wise people, he would never have fallen into that misfortune; for he himself was good and wise

~

Henry V:

Fortune is painted blind, with a muffler afore her eyes, to signify to you that Fortune is blind; and she is painted also with a wheel, to signify to you, which is the moral of it, that she is turning, and inconstant, and mutability, and variation; and her foot, look you, is fixed upon a spherical stone, which rolls, and rolls, and rolls. In good truth, the poet makes a most excellent description of it: Fortune is an excellent moral

Bacon, "Of Fortune":

If a man look sharply and attentively, he shall see Fortune; for though she is blind, she is not invisible

Anatomie of the Minde:

The Philosophers, and other unfaithful heathens, considering the mutability of all things, and the small assurance that man hath of anything, have supposed this world to be governed by some blind or beastly God. And hereof came the fiction of Fortune, which is of ancients, both Poets and painters feigned to be blind, brutish and frantic, and so to stand upon a round stone, distributing worldly things. She is thought to be blind, because she bestows her gifts without consideration of Persons; Brutish, because she rewards most commonly, the most ungodly; without judgement, Mad, because she is wayward, cruel and inconstant; standing not upon a square stone, for that abides, but upon a round one, for that slides continually. And therefore she is counted as brittle as glass, and nothing or more unstable. And yet notwithstanding, at her pleasure she bestows all things; which Virgil confirms, for he ascribes unto her this title Omnipotent; and Sallust says, that in all things Fortune bears sway. But let them as Heathens, and without the knowledge of the true God, imagine what they list, yet let us think, and believe none to be Omnipotent, and to dispose the world, and that which is in the same, but only our God, not Fortune; and that he does all things, not rashly without reason, but providently to our preservation; and that he is not mad in his doings, but mighty and marvelous, and doth all things to the comfort of his elect

Anti-Machiavel:

the pagan poets have written that Fortune is a goddess who gives good and evil things to whom she will. And to denote that she does this inconsiderately and without judgment, they wrap her head in a cloth, lest with her eyes she sees and knows to whom she gives; so that she never knows unto whom she does good or evil. Moreover, they describe her standing upright upon a bowl, to denote her inconstancy, turning and tossing from side to side. Now Machiavelli would make men believe that this is true, and that all the good and evil which comes to men happens because they have Fortune accordant or discordant to their complexions. He says that she commonly favors young people, such as are hazardous and inconsiderate; to the end that thereby men might learn to be rash, violent, and heady, that they may have Fortune favorable to them. But all this doctrine tends to the same end as the former maxims do, to insinuate into men's minds and hearts a spite and utter contempt of God and his providence. For let man have once this persuasion, that no good comes to us from God, but from Fortune, he will easily forsake the service of God

By this description of Machiavelli is evidently seen that he thinks what the poets wrote for fables concerning fortune is the very truth. For the pagan poets have written that fortune is a goddess who gives good and evil things to whom she will. And to denote that she does this inconsiderately and without judgment, they wrap her head in a cloth, lest with her eyes she sees and knows to whom she gives; so that she never knows unto whom she does good or evil. Moreover, they describe her standing upright upon a bowl, to denote her inconstancy, turning and tossing from side to side. . . For certain it is that the haps which men call

Fortune proceed from God, who rather blesses prudence, which he has recommended unto us, than temerity. And although it sometimes happens that he blesses not our counsels and wisdoms, it is because we take them not from the true spring and fountain, namely from him of whom we ought to have asked it; and that most commonly we would rather our own wisdom be a glory unto us, whereas only God should be glorified

3. *The French Academy*

L'Academie Française was published in four volumes from 1578-98 and in English translation from 1584-1618. It has numerous parallels with *The Anatomie of the Minde* and *Anti-Machiavel*, and resembles Francis Bacon's *Essays*, bearing titles "Of Ambition," "Of Hope," "Of Prosperity and Adversity," etc. As with Shakespeare's *Love's Labour's Lost*, it features four young French gentlemen secluded for purposes of study. In the dedication to Henri III, the author speaks of having attended the Estates General in 1576-7, as did Bacon. He begins: "Sir, if we credit the saying of Plato, commonwealths begin then to be happy, when kings exercise philosophy, and philosophers reign." *Anti-Machiavel*:

> there cannot come a better and more profitable thing to a people than to have a prince wise of himself; therefore, said Plato, men may call it a happy commonwealth when either the prince can play the philosopher, or when a philosopher comes to reign there

Bacon's *Advancement of Learning*:

> although he might be thought partial to his own profession, that said 'then should people and estates be happy, when either kings were philosophers, or philosophers kings'; yet so much is verified by experience, that under learned princes and governors there have ever been the best times

As an example, *The French Academy* cites "Francis I, a prince of most famous memory, [who] so loved and favored letters and the professors of them that he deserved the name of the restorer of sciences and good arts" (in the Introduction we noted that the *History of the Royal Society* (1667) depicted Bacon as *Artium Instaurator*, "restorer of the arts"). *Anti-Machiavel* said "the restoration of good letters, which Francis I brought into France, did more to celebrate and immortalize his name in the memory of all Christian nations, than all the great wars and victories his predecessors had."

As with *Anti-Machiavel*, *The French Academy* attributes France's troubles to foreign influence:

> the ruin and destruction of this French monarchy proceeds of no other second cause (our iniquity being the first) than of the mixture which we have made of strangers with ourselves. Wherein we are not contented to seek them out under their roofs, unless we also draw them unto us and

lodge them under our roofs, yea prefer them before our own countrymen and citizens in the offices and honorable places of this kingdom

An English intelligence paper sometimes credited to Francis (or Anthony) Bacon, "Notes on the Present State of Christendom" (1582), reported

> division in [France] for matters of religion and state, through miscontentment of the nobility to see strangers advanced to the greatest charges of the realm, the offices of justice sold, the treasury wasted, the people polled, the country destroyed, hath bred great trouble, and like to see more

Anti-Machiavel complains of "all France fashioned after the manners, conditions, and vices of foreigners that govern it, and who have the principal charges and estates." Shakespeare's *Richard II* laments

> Reports of fashions in proud Italy
> Whose manners still our tardy-apish nation
> Limps after in base imitation.
> Where the world doth thrust forth a vanity—
> So be it new, there's no respect how vile

The French Academy warns: "It is a hard matter (said Socrates) for a man to bridle his desire, but he that addeth riches thereunto, is mad." *Anti-Machiavel* asked: "Who could then bridle vices and iniquities, which are fed with much wealth, and no less liberty?" Bacon's *New Atlantis* again echoes: "the reverence of a man's self is, next religion, the chiefest bridle of all vices." Finally, *The French Academy* echoes the strident tone as well as the content of *Anti-Machiavel*:

> there are a great many amongst us of those foolish men of whom David speaks, *Who say in their hearts that there is no God*. In the forefront of which company, the students of Machiavel's principles and practicers of his precepts may worthily be ranged. This bad fellow, whose works are no less accounted of among his followers than were Apollo's Oracles amongst the Heathen, nay than the sacred Scriptures are among sound Christians, blushed not to belch out these horrible blasphemies against pure religion, and so against God the Author thereof; namely, that the religion of the heathen made them stout and courageous, whereas Christian religion makes the professors thereof base minded, timorous, and fit to become a prey to every one; that since men fell from the religion of the Heathen, they became so corrupt that they would believe neither God nor the Devil; that Moses so possessed the land of Judea as the Goths did by strong hand usurp part

of the Roman Empire. These and such like positions are spewed out by this hell hound sometimes against true religion, other whiles against the religion and Church of Rome, sometimes also taxing the religion of the heathen of falsehood and cozenage; so that in truth he would have all religion to be of like account with his disciples, except it be so far forth as the pretense and show of religion may serve to set forward and effect their wicked policies. And for this cause he sets down this rule for every Prince and Magistrate to frame his religion by, namely, that he should pretend to be very religious and devout, although it be but in hypocrisy. And to this he adds a second precept no less impious, that a Prince should with tooth and nail maintain false miracles and untruths in religion, so long as his people may thereby be kept in greater obedience.

Parallelisms

As You Like It:

> All the world's a stage,
> And all the men and women merely players:
> They have their exits and entrances;
> And one man in his time plays many parts,
> His acts being seven ages.

French Academy:

Now, among them that have most diligently observed the secrets of man's nature, there have been two sundry opinions concerning the division of the ages of man. Some have made seven parts, adding decrepit or bedridden age after old age, and they would ground their principal reason of this division upon this, that the number of seven is a universal and absolute number.

∼

French Academy:

These are those good reasons, which ought to sound often in the ears of young men, and be supplied little by little through the study of good letters, and Moral Philosophy of ancient men, until they have wholly in possession that place of manners, which is soonest moved and most easily led, and are lodged therein by knowledge and judgement, which will be as a guard to preserve and defend that age from corruption

Troilus and Cressida:

not much unlike young men, whom Aristotle thought unfit to hear moral philosophy. The reasons you allege do more conduce to the hot passions of distermper'd blood than to make up a free determination 'twixt right and wrong.

Advancement of Learning:

Is not the opinion of Aristotle worthy to be regarded wherein he saith that young men are no fit auditors of moral philosophy, because they are not settled from the boiling heat of their affections, nor attempered with time and experience.

∼

Much Ado About Nothing:

There was never yet philosopher
That could endure the toothache patiently,
However they have writ the style of the Gods,
And made a push at chance and sufferance.

Bacon, letter to the Earl of Essex:

It is more than a philosopher morally can digest… I esteem it like the pulling out of an aching tooth, which I remember when I was a child and had a little philosophy, I was glad when it was done.

Bacon, "Of Anger":

To seek to extinguish anger utterly is but a bravery of the Stoics. We have better oracles: Be angry, but sin not: let not the sun go down on your anger.

French Academy:

Among all the ancients, the Stoic Philosophers were most zealous and precise observers of all points concerning this virtue of patience; which they grounded upon the fatal cause of necessity, requiring such exactness and perfection thereof in men, that they would have a noble heart to be no otherwise touched with adversity than with prosperity, nor with sorrowful things than with joyful. For this cause Aristotle said that virtue only was to be wished; and therefore that it was all one to be sick or sound, poor or rich; briefly, that in all other human and necessary uses of nature, there was no more evil in one kind than in another. Whereby it seems that these Philosophers delighted in painting out a picture of such patience as never was, nor shall be among men, except first they should be unclothed of all human nature, or become as blockish and senseless as a stone.

~

French Academy:

And as the heat buried in the veins of a flint seems rather dead than alive, if the sparkles be not drawn forth by the steel, so this immortal portion of celestial fire, being the fountain and first motive of all knowledge, remains without any profit or commendable action, if it be not sharpened and set on work.

Timon of Athens:

> The fire i' the flint
> Shows not till it be struck; our gentle flame
> Provokes itself and like the current flies
> Each bound it chafes.

Troilus and Cressida:

> There were wit in this head, and 'twould
> Out" – and so there is, but it lies as coldly in him as
> fire in a flint, which will not show without knocking.

Julius Caesar:

> O Cassius, you are yoked with a lamb
> That carries anger as the flint bears fire,
> Who, much enforced, shows a hasty spark,
> And straight is cold again.

~

French Academy:

Thales said that nothing in all the world was more common than Hope, because it abides with them also that have no other goods.

Measure for Measure:

> The miserable have no other medicine but only hope

~

French Academy:

Samson betrayed by Dalilah, Solomon became brutish through his concubines, Ahab rooted out through Jezebel, Mark Antony slew himself for the love of Cleopatra, the destruction of Troy because of Helena, the Pandora of Hesiod, the pitiful death of Hercules by Deiamra, and many other miserable events procured chiefly by women, and plentifully declared in histories

Love's Labour's Lost:

Love is a devil. There is not evil angel but Love. Yet was Samson so tempted, and he had an excellent strength; yet was Solomon so seduced, and he had a very good wit. Cupid's butt shaft is too hard for Hercules' club, and therefore too much odds for a Spaniard's rapier

~

French Academy:

Thales, one of the Sages of Greece, minding to show that it was not good for a man to marry when one asked him why he married not, being in the flower of his age, said that it was not yet time. Afterward, being grown to further age and demanded the same question, he answered, that the time was past.

Bacon, *Apophthegms*:

Thales being asked when a man should marry, said young men not yet, old men not at all

French Academy:

And to those whose minds are not well disposed, neither riches, nor strength, nor beauty can be judged good, but the greater increase arises of them, the more harm they may procure to him that possesses them

As You Like It:

Know you not, master, to some kind of men their graces serve them but as enemies? No more do yours; your virtues, gentle master, are sanctified and holy traitors to you. Oh, what a world is this, when what is comely envenoms him that bears it!

French Academy:

Was there ever any captain among the Romans greater than Julius Caesar? Yet was he of a weak and tender complexion, subject to great headaches, and visited sometimes with the falling sickness.

Julius Caesar:

> *Casca.* He fell down in the market-place, and foam'd at the mouth, and was speechless.
>
> *Brutus.* 'Tis very like; he hath the falling-sickness.

As You Like It:

> Your "if" is the only peacemaker; much virtue in "if."

French Academy:

And when they were to answer anything propounded on a sudden, avoiding all superfluous speech, their answers were very witty and well contrived, their words very significant and short, having in them both grace and gravity joined together. As when Philip king of Macedonia wrote unto them, that if he entered within Laconia, he would overthrow them topsy-turvy; they wrote back unto him only this word, If.

French Academy:

This was wisely noted by Philippides, when Lysimachus the king asked him what part of his goods he would have imparted unto him. "What you please Sir" (said he), "so it be no part of your secrets."

Pericles:

Well, I perceive he was a wise fellow and had good discretion that, being bid to ask what he would of the King, desired he might know none of his secrets.

Troilus and Cressida:

> They tax our policy and call it cowardice,
> Count wisdom as no member of the war,
> Forestall prescience, and esteem no act
> But that of hand. The still and mental parts
> That do contrive how many hands shall strike
> When fitness calls them on and know by measure
> Of their observant toil the enemy's weight –
> Why, this hath not a finger's dignity.
> They call this bed work, mappery, closet war;
> So that the ram that batters down the wall,
> For the great swinge and rudeness of his poise,
> They place before his hand that made the engine,
> Or those that with the fineness of their souls
> By reason guide his execution.

French Academy:

Fabius the Greatest comes first to my remembrance, to prove that the resolution of a courageous heart, grounded upon knowledge and the discourse of reason, is firm and immutable. This Captain of the Roman army, being sent into the field to resist the fury and violence of Hannibal, who being Captain of the Carthaginians, was entered into Italy with great force, determined for the public welfare and necessity to delay and prolong the war, and not to hazard a battle but with great advantage. Whereupon certain told him that his own men called him Hannibal's schoolmaster, and that he was jested at with many other opprobrious speeches, as one that had small valor and courage in him; and therefore they counseled him to fight, to the end he might not incur any more such reprehensions and obloquies. I should be (said he again to them) a greater coward than now I am thought to be, if I should forsake my deliberation necessary for the common welfare and safety, for fear of their girding speeches and bolts of mockery, and obey those (to the ruin of my country) whom I ought to command. And indeed afterward he gave great tokens of his unspeakable valor, being sent with three hundred men only to encounter with the said Hannibal; and seeing that he must of necessity fight for the safety of the Commonwealth, after all his men were slain, and himself hurt to death, he rushed against Hannibal with so great violence and force of courage, that he took from him the diadem or frontlet, which he had about his head, and died with that about him.

∼

French Academy:

As the remembrance of an evil is kept a long time, because that which offends is very hardly forgotten, so we commonly see that the memory of benefits received is as suddenly vanished and lost, as the fruit of the good turn is perceived.

Troilus and Cressida:

> Time hath, my lord, a wallet at his back,
> Wherein he puts alms for oblivion,
> A great-sized monster of ingratitudes.
> Those scraps are good deeds past, which are devoured
> As fast as they are made, forgot as soon
> As done.

∼

French Academy:

This is that which Possidonius teaches us, saying that anger is nothing else but a short fury.

Timon of Athens:

> They say, my lords, "*Ira furor brevis est*";
> But yond man is ever angry.

~

French Academy:

Timon the Athenian, detesting much more than all these the imbecility of man's nature, used and employed all his skill to persuade his countrymen to abridge and shorten the course of their so miserable life, and to hasten their end by hanging themselves upon gibbets, which he had caused to set up in great number, in a field that he bought for the same purpose, unto whose persuasions many gave place.

Timon of Athens:

> Tell my friends,
> Tell Athens, in the sequence of degree
> From high to low throughout, that whoso please
> To stop affliction, let him take his haste,
> Come hither ere my tree hath felt the ax,
> And hang himself.

~

French Academy:

But to the end we confound not together that which is simply divine, with that which is human, I think we ought to make a double hope; the first true, certain, and infallible, which concerns holy and sacred mysteries; the other doubtful, respecting earthly things only.

Troilus and Cressida:

> The ample proposition that hope makes
> In all designs begun on earth below
> Fails in the promised largeness. Checks and disasters
> Grow in the veins of actions highest reared,
> As knots, by the conflux of meeting sap,
> Infects the sound pine and diverts his grain
> Tortive and errant from his course of growth.

French Academy:

Sir, if we credit the saying of Plato, commonwealths begin then to be happy, when kings exercise philosophy, and philosophers reign.

Anti-Machiavel:

I am content to presuppose that it is certain that there cannot come a better and more profitable thing to a people than to have a prince wise of himself; therefore, said Plato, men may call it a happy commonwealth when either the prince can play the philosopher, or when a philosopher comes to reign there.

French Academy:

The desire which Plato had to profit many caused him to sail from Greece into Sicily, that by grave discourses and wise instructions he might stay and contain within the bounds of reason the young years of Dionysius, prince of that country, who through unbridled liberty and power not limited waved hither and thither without restraint. Afterward, when he began to be in love with the beauty of learning, he left off little by little his drunkenness, maskings, and whoredoms, wherein before he gloried; insomuch that his court was wholly changed upon a sudden, as if it had been inspired from heaven. But within a while after, Dionysius giving ear to flatterers, banished Plato; to whom when he took his leave of him, the tyrant said, I doubt not, Plato, but you will speak ill of me when you are in the University among thy companions and friends. Whereupon the philosopher smiling and observing that freedom of speech which he had always used towards him, made this answer. I pray God, Sir, there may never be so great want of matter to speak of in the University, that we need to speak of thee.

Anatomie of the Minde:

It is written of Dionysius, a most cruel tyrant, that as long as he perceived himself to be well reported of, he was a good man, but when the privy talk to his defamation came to his ears, he then began to leave his good nature, and to exercise all kind of cruelty toward his subjects, and became the most cruel Prince that ever was.

French Academy:

It is a hard matter (said Socrates) for a man to bridle his desire, but he that addeth riches therunto, is mad.

Anti-Machiavel:

Who could then bridle vices and iniquities, which are fed with much wealth, and no less liberty?

French Academy:

He that has but half an eye may see that there are a great many amongst us of those foolish men of whom David speaks, *Who say in their hearts that there is no God*. In the forefront of which company, the students of Machiavel's principles and practicers of his precepts may worthily be ranged. This bad fellow, whose works are no less accounted of among his followers than were Apollo's oracles amongst the heathen, nay than the sacred Scriptures are among sound Christians, blushed not to belch out these horrible blasphemies against pure religion, and so against God the author thereof…

Anti-Machiavel:

For what shall I speak of religion, whereof the Machiavellians had none, as already plainly appears; yet they greatly labored also to deprive us of the same… he is of no reputation in the court of France who has not Machiavelli's writings at the fingers' ends, both in the Italian and French tongues, and can apply his precepts to all purposes, as the oracles of Apollo.

French Academy:

For the ruin and destruction of this French monarchy proceeds of no other second cause (our iniquity being the first) than of the mixture which we have made of strangers with ourselves. Wherein we are not contented to seek them out under their roofs, unless we also draw them unto us and lodge them under our roofs, yea prefer them before our own countrymen and citizens in the offices and honorable places of this kingdom… they have left us nothing but new manners and fashions of living in all dissoluteness and pleasure; except this one thing also, that we have learned of them to dissemble, and withal to frame and build a treason very subtly. Such is the provision wherewith our French youth is commonly furnished by their Italian voyages.

Anti-Machiavel:

For besides the examples we read in histories, we know it by experience, seeing at this day all France fashioned after the manners, conditions, and vices of foreigners that govern it, and who have the principal charges and estates. And not only many Frenchmen are such beasts to conform themselves to strangers' complexions, but also to gaggle their language and disdain the French tongue as a thing too common and vulgar.

∼

French Academy:

This is that which at length (as Crates the philosopher said very well) stirs up civil wars, seditions, and tyrannies within cities; to the end that such voluptuous men, and ambitious of vainglory, fishing in a troubled water, may have wherewith to maintain their foolish expenses, and so come to the end of their platforms.

Anti-Machiavel:

And would to God that the French nation had never been of that nature and condition to do well unto strangers, without first knowing and trying their behaviors and manner of life. We should not then see France to be governed and ruled by strangers, as it is; we should not feel the calamities and troubles of civil wars and dissentions, which they enterprise to maintain their greatness and magnitude, and to fish in troubled water.

∼

French Academy:

But whatsoever my speech has been hitherto, my meaning is not to find fault with the right use of hospitality, which ought to be maintained and kept inviolable in every well-established commonwealth. In this respect France has been commended above all nations for entertaining and receiving all sorts of people; provided always that they be not preferred before our own children, and that they be contented to obey and live according to the common laws of the country.

Anti-Machiavel:

For hospitality is recommended unto us by God, and it is a very laudable virtue for men to entertain strangers and entertain them well; but strangers also ought to content themselves to be welcomed and entertained in a country or town, without aspiring to master or hold offices and estates. The French nation is that which of all Christendom receives and loves strangers most, for they are as welcome all over France as those of their own nation.

~

French Academy:

What ought they to do, that say they are all members of that one head, who recommends so expressly unto them meekness, mildness, gentleness, grace, clemency, mercy, good will, compassion, and every good affection towards their neighbor? All which things are comprehended under this only sacred word of Charity

Anti-Machiavel:

True charity is joined unto faith, pity, and all other virtues

~

French Academy:

Notwithstanding, wisely applying themselves to places and persons, they can in their serious discourses intermingle some honest pastimes, but yet not altogether without profit. As Plato in his foresaid feast interlaces certain comical speeches of love, howbeit all the rest of the supper there was nothing but wise discourses of philosophy.

Anti-Machiavel:

But seeing we are entered into this talk, we will look deeper into the matter to draw out some good resolution from this question, by the way only of a tentative and pleasant disputation, and not of a full determination hereof. For as Cato says, amongst serious things joyous and merry things would be sometimes mixed.

French Academy:

Kings, princes and magistrates, who because they see and hear for the most part by other men's eyes and ears, ought necessarily to have such friends, counsellors, and servants about them, as will freely tell them the truth, as hereafter we may discourse more at large.

Anti-Machiavel:

And to attend while the prince himself begins the matter first to his council, would be in vain; for he cannot propose what he does not know, and it is a notorious and plain thing that the prince, who is always shut up in a house or within a troupe of his people, sees not nor knows how things pass, but what men make him see and know.

~

French Academy:

Francis I, a prince of most famous memory, so loved and favored letters and the professors of them that he deserved the name of the restorer of sciences and good arts, sparing neither care nor means to assemble together books and volumes of sundry sorts and of all languages for the beautifying of his so renowned a library, which was a worthy monument of such a magnifical Monarch; whose praiseworthy qualities we see revived in our king, treading in the selfsame steps.

Anti-Machiavel:

We see that the restoration of good letters, which Francis I brought into France, did more to celebrate and immortalize his name in the memory of all Christian nations, than all the great wars and victories his predecessors had… In our time Francis I imitated the example of this great and wise emperor, establishing public lectures at great wages in the University of Paris, a thing whereof his memory has been and shall be more celebrated through the world than for so many great wars he valiantly sustained during his reign… You have gloriously crowned that work, which that great king Francis your grandfather did happily begin, to the end that arts and sciences might flourish in this kingdom.

~

French Academy:

It is a usual speech in the mouths of men altogether ignorant of the beauty and profit of Sciences, that the study of letters is a bottomless gulf, and so long and uneasy a journey that they who think to finish it, oftentimes stay in the midway, and many being come to the end thereof find their minds so confused with their profound and curious skill, that instead of tranquility of soul, which they thought to find, they have increased the trouble of their spirit.

Anti-Machiavel:

For there are at this day infinite persons who so much please themselves in profane authors, some in poets, some in historiographers, some in philosophy, some in physic, or in law, that they care nothing to read or else to know anything for the salvation and comfort of their souls. Some care not at all for it, others reserve that study until they have ended the studies of other sciences, and in the meanwhile the time runs away, and often it comes to pass that when they leave this world, their profane studies are not ended, nor the study of holy letters commenced, and so they die like beasts.

∼

French Academy:

Through want of skill and ignorance he falls into a worse estate than he was in before, and as we commonly say, from a gentle ague into a pestilent and burning fever

Anti-Machiavel:

They were fallen from a shaking fever into a hot ague, as the French proverb is

∼

French Academy:

Whereunto also the precepts and discourses of learned and ancient philosophers may serve for our instruction and pricking forward; as also the examples (which are lively reasons) of the lives of so many notable men, as histories, the mother of antiquity, do as it were represent alive before our eyes.

Anti-Machiavel:

And you, good Edward, imitate the wisdom, sanctimony, and integrity of your father, the Right Honorable Lord Nicholas Bacon, Keeper of the broad Seal of England, a man right renowned; that you may lively express the image of your father's virtues in the excellent towardness which you naturally have from your most virtuous father. If you both daily ruminate and remember the familiar and best known examples of your ancestors, you cannot have more forcible persuasions to move you to that which is good and honest.

∼

French Academy:

If we compare worldly goods with virtue (calling that good which usurps that name, and is subject to corruption); first, as touching those which the philosophers call the goods of fortune, and namely nobility, whereon at this day men stay so much; what is it but a good of our ancestors?

Anti-Machiavel:

I will also note another notable vice which runs current among gentlemen at this day, which is that they make so great account of their nobility of blood that they esteem not the nobility of virtue; insomuch that it seems to some that no vices can dishonor or pollute the nobility and gentry which they have from their ancestors. But they ought well to consider that to their race there was a beginning of nobility, which was attributed to the first that was noble in consideration of some virtue that was in him.

∼

French Academy:

Ambition truly is the most vehement and strongest passion of all those wherewith men's minds are troubled; and yet many notable and virtuous men have so mastered it by the force of their temperance that oftentimes they accepted offices and estates of supreme authority, as it were by compulsion and with grief; yea some altogether contemned and willingly forsook them.

Anti-Machiavel:

Besides all this, in the election of counsellors and magistrates he did ever suspect those who sought offices, and held them for ambitious and dangerous people to the common weal. But they who he could know to be good men and worthy of public charge, and never sought it, these were they who he esteemed most sufficient; and the more they excused themselves from accepting offices, so much the more were they constrained unto them.

~

French Academy:

The custom that Aurelius Severus used is much more praiseworthy. For when he sent governors into the provinces, he caused their names to be published many days before, to the end that whosoever knew anything in them worthy of reprehension, he should give notice thereof; and they that reported truly, were promoted to honor by him and slanderers grievously punished.

Anti-Machiavel:

And upon that point, it seems to me that the manner of proceeding which Alexander Severus used to choose his counsellors and his magistrates, is very good and merits well to be imitated and drawn into consequence… And the better to be informed of the reputation of persons whereof he had proffers by his wise friends, he caused to be set up in common streets and great public areas, where many ways meet, certain posts to fix bills upon them, whereupon was written certain exhortations unto the people, that if any man had anything to say against such and such a man (which he named) wherefore they might not be received and admitted to such and such an office, that he should denounce it. And so made those commands by placards, to the end he might better discover and be advertised of the virtues and vices of persons.

~

French Academy:

Caligula, a most cruel emperor, never had secure and quiet rest, but being terrified and in fear awoke often, as one that was vexed and carried headlong with wonderful passions. Nero, after he had killed his mother, confessed that while he slept he was troubled by her, and tormented with Furies that burned him with flaming torches.

Anti-Machiavel:

What repose could Nero have, who confessed that often the likeness of his mother, whom he slew, appeared to him, which tormented and afflicted him; and that the furies beat him with rods and tormented him with burning torches. What delicateness or sweetness of life could Caligula and Caracalla have? who always carried coffers full of all manners of poisons, as well to poison others as themselves in case of necessity, for fear they should fall alive into the hands of their enemies.

∼

Anti-Machiavel:

The governor of Judea, called Petronius, would have placed an image of Caligula in the great temple of Jerusalem; but the Jews, who extremely detested images, would not suffer him; whereby there was likely to have been a great sedition.

French Academy:

Caligula, a Roman emperor, sent Petronius into Syria with commandment to make war with the Jews if they would not receive his image into their temple. Which when they refused to do, Petronius said unto them that then belike they would fight against Caesar, not weighing his wealth or their own weaknesses and inability.

∼

French Academy:

Alexander the Great, being by the states of all Greece chosen general captain to pass into Asia and to make war with the Persians, before he took ship he inquired after the estate of all his friends to know what means they had to follow him. Then he distributed and gave to one lands, to another a village, to this man the custom of some haven, to another the profit of some borough town, bestowing in this manner the most part of his demeans and revenues. And when Perdicas, one of his lieutenants, demanded of him what he reserved for himself: he answered Hope.

Anti-Machiavel:

When Alexander the Great departed from Macedonia to go to the conquest of Asia, he had all the captains of his army appear before him and distributed to them almost all the revenue of his kingdom, leaving himself almost nothing. One of the captains, named Perdicas, said to him: "What then will you keep for yourself?" "Even hope," answered Alexander.

~

French Academy:

Anaxarchus the philosopher, being taken prisoner by the commandment of Nero, that he might know of him who were the authors of a conspiracy that was made against his estate, and being led towards him for the same cause, he bit his tongue in sunder with his teeth and spit in his face, knowing well that otherwise the tyrant would have compelled him by all sorts of tortures and torments to reveal and disclose them. Zeno missing his purpose, which was to have killed the tyrant Demylus, did as much to him.

The Anatomie of the Minde:

Zeno the Stoic being cruelly tormented of a King of Cypress to utter those things which the king was desirous to know, at length because he would not satisfy his mind, bit off his own tongue, and spit the same in the tormentor's face. But the constancy of Anaxarchus was more strange, for being taken of Nicocreon, a most cruel of all other Tyrants, and afterward hearing that by the commandment of the Tyrant he should in a mortar he bruised and broken into pieces, said most constantly unto him in this manner; Bruise and break this body of mine at thy pleasure O Tyrant, yet shalt thou never diminish any whit of Anaxarchus. Then the Tyrant because he could not abide his bold speech, commanded that his tongue should be cut out of his mouth. But Anaxarchus laughing at his madness, thought he should never have his mind, and therefore he bit out his own tongue and spit the same by mammocks upon the tyrant's face.

~

Anatomie of the Minde:

what so savage as Xerxes, which appointed a great reward unto him, which invented a new pleasure never heard of before?

French Academy:

Xerxes, monarch of the Persians, was so intemperate and given to lust that he propounded rewards for those that could invent some new kind of pleasure; and therefore coming into Greece with an infinite number of men to subdue it, he was overcome and repulsed by a small number, as being an effeminate and fainthearted man.

~

French Academy:

Fabius the Greatest comes first to my remembrance, to prove that the resolution of a courageous heart, grounded upon knowledge and the discourse of reason, is firm and immutable. This captain of the Roman army being sent into the field to resist the fury and violence of Hannibal, who being captain of the Carthaginians, was entered into Italy with great force, determined for the public welfare and necessity to delay and prolong the war, and not to hazard a battle but with great advantage.

Anti-Machiavel:

Seeing this, the Roman Senate sent against Hannibal Fabius Maximus, who was not so forward (and it may be not so hardy) as Flaminius or Sempronius were; but he was more wise and careful, as he showed himself. On his arrival he did not set upon Hannibal, who desired no other thing, but began to coast him far off, seeking always advantageous places. And when Hannibal approached him, then would he show him a countenance fully determined to fight, yet always seeking places of advantage. But Hannibal, who was not so rash as to join with his enemy to his own disadvantage, made a show to recoil and fly, to draw him after him. Fabius followed him, but upon coasts and hills, seeking always not the shortest way, but that way which was most for his advantage.

~

French Academy:

Scipio Africanus, general of the Romans, at the taking of the city of Carthage had a young damsel taken prisoner, of rare and excellent beauty. And when he understood of what great calling she came, and how her parents not long before had betrothed her to a great lord of Spain, he commanded that he should be sent for, and restored her unto him without abusing her in any respect, although he was in the flower of his age and had free and sovereign authority. Moreover, he gave for a dowry with her the money that was brought unto him for her ransom.

Anti-Machiavel:

Yet the example of clemency in Scipio Africanus is more notable than this of his father and uncle. After the deaths of his said father and uncle, this young lord full of all generosity and hardiness came to besiege New Carthage in Spain, and got it by assault… Among other hostages, there was a young lady of a great house brought to Scipio, who was of so great beauty that as she passed by she drew each man's regard upon her. This lady was affianced to one Allucius, prince of the Celts. Scipio, taking knowledge of her parents and to whom she was affianced, and that Allucius extremely loved her, sent for them all… The said lady's parents stepped forward and presented to him a great quantity of gold and silver for their daughter's ransom, which though Scipio refused it, they pressed it so sore upon him that he accorded to take it, and bade them lay it before him. Scipio called Allucius and said to him, Good friend, besides the dowry which your father-in-law will give you, my desire is that you will take this silver at my hands as an increase of her dowry.

~

French Academy:

Camillus, a Roman dictator, is no less to be commended for that which he did during the siege of the City of the Fallerians. For he that was schoolmaster of the chiefest men's children among them, being gone out of the city, under color to have his youth to walk and to exercise themselves along the walls, delivered them into the hands of the Roman captain; saying unto him that he might be well assured the citizens would yield themselves to his devotion, for the safety and liberty of that which was dearest unto them. But Camillus, knowing this to be too vile and wicked a practice, said to those that were with him, that although men used great outrage and violence in war, yet among good men certain laws and points of equity were to be observed. For victory was not so much to be desired, as that it should be gotten and kept by such cursed and damnable means; but a general ought to war, trusting to his own virtue, and not to the wickedness of others. Then stripping the said schoolmaster, and bending his hands behind him, he delivered him naked into the hands of his scholars, and gave to each of them a bundle of rods, that so they might carry him back again into the city. For which noble act the citizens yielded themselves to the Romans, saying that in preferring justice before victory, they had taught them to choose rather to submit themselves unto them, than to retain still their liberty; confessing withal that they were overcome more by their virtue than vanquished by their force and power.

Anti-Machiavel:

Camillus, a Roman general, besieged the town of Falisques, the Romans' enemies. The schoolmaster of Falisques enterprised a great wickedness and villainy; for making a countenance to lead, for sport and pastime, the youth of that town who were committed to him to be instructed, he straight brought them to Camillus' camp, hoping he would give some good recompense, speaking in this manner. "Lord Camillus, I yield into your hands the town of Falisques, for I here bring you their dear and loving children, which to recover they will easily yield themselves to you." To whom Camillus answered, "Wicked wretch, you do not address yourself to your like. We have by compacts no society with the Falisques, but by nature we have; we are not ignorant of the right of war and of peace, which we will courageously observe. We make not war upon young children, for even when we take towns, we pardon them, so do we also to them who bear arms against us. You would vanquish the Falisques by deceit and villainy, but I will vanquish them by virtue and arms, as I overcame the Veians." After this, Camillus commanded to bind the schoolmaster's hands behind him, and to give all the scholars rods in their hands, who whipped him naked into the town. As thus in this sort the children brought their master to the town, all the people ran to see the spectacle; which so changed their courage, before full of wrath and hatred against the Romans, that they straight sent delegates to Camillus to desire peace, admiring the Roman clemency and justice. Camillus, knowing that he alone could not enterprise to conclude a peace, sent the delegates towards the Senate of Rome, where on arriving they made this speech. "My masters, having been vanquished by an agreeable victory both to gods and men, we yield ourselves to you, knowing that our estate shall be better under your domination than in our own liberties and customs. The issue of this war will serve hereafter for a double example to all mankind, for it seems you better love loyalty in war than present victory. And we, being provoked by your kindness and loyalty, gladly and willingly yield you the victory. We offer ourselves your subjects, and we shall never repent ourselves of your domination, nor you of your loyalty." The peace and alliance accorded to the Falisques, Camillus entered Rome in triumph, and was more esteemed to be a victor by clemency than if it had been by arms.

~

French Academy:

Caracalla the emperor, traveling with his army towards the Parthians, under pretense of marrying the daughter of Artabanus their king, who came for the same purpose to meet him, he set upon him contrary to his faith, and put him to flight with an incredible murder of his men. But within a while after, being come down from his horse to make water, he was slain by his own men; which was noted as a just punishment sent from God for his unfaithfulness.

Anti-Machiavel:

[Caracalla] also played another part of treachery, under the pretext and show of marriage, with Artabanus, king of the Parthians. For he wrote letters to him whereby he signified that their empires were the two greatest empires of the world; and that being the son of a Roman emperor, he could not find a better wife than the daughter of the king of the Parthians. He therefore asked her hand in marriage, to join the greatest empires of the earth and to end their wars. The king at first denied Caracalla his daughter, saying that such a marriage was very unfit because of the diversity of their languages, manners, and habits; also because the Romans had never before allied or married with the Parthians. But upon this refusal Caracalla insisted and pressed him more strongly than before, and sent to Artabanus great gifts, so that in the end he gave to him his daughter. Caracalla, assuring himself that he would find no hostility in the Parthian country, boldly entered far into it with his army, saying he went but to see the king's daughter. On the other side, Artabanus prepared himself and his retinue in as good order as was possible, without any army, to go meet his new son-in-law. What did this perfidious Caracalla? As soon as the two parties met, and Artabanus came near to salute and embrace him, he commanded his soldiers to charge upon the Parthians. The Romans attacked as if there had been an assigned battle, and there was a great slaughter made of the Parthians; but the king, with the help of a good horse, escaped with great difficulty and danger. He determined to revenge himself of that villainy and treachery; but Macrinus relieved him of that pain, and soon slew that monster Caracalla, who was already detested through all the world because of his perfidy.

~

French Academy:

Antoninus and Geta, brothers and successors in the empire to Severus their father, could not suffer one another to enjoy so large a monarchy; for Antoninus slew his brother Geta with a dagger, that himself might rule alone.

Anti-Machiavel:

Severus intending to leave the government of the empire to his two sons together, flatterers about them disposed it otherwise… Those two young princes fell into so great and mortal enmity, that not only they hated all each other's friends and servants, but also those who would have reconciled them. As soon as their father Severus was dead, Laetus, one of the marmosets of Bassianus, persuaded him to slay his brother and feign that he was assailed by him. This counsel was found good by Bassianus, who was audacious enough and ready to give the blow with his own hand. One morning he entered into the chamber of empress Julia, Geta's mother, and finding him there he slew him between his mother's arms.

~

French Academy:

And it is greatly to be feared that such unskillful and ambitious men will in the end show themselves both in will and practice to be imitators of one Cleander, an outlandish slave, who being preferred by Commodus the emperor to goodly offices and great places of honor, as to be great master of his men of war and his chief chamberlain, conspired notwithstanding against his lord, seeking to attain to the imperial dignity by seditions which he stirred up in Rome between the people and the soldiers. But through good order taken, his enterprise took no effect, except the loss of his own head and destruction of his house.

Anti-Machiavel:

Cleander was another marmoset who succeeded in his place; who at the beginning made some show that he would do better, but soon did worse. He practiced many cruelties, and sold the estates and governments of provinces to those who would offer most. There happened at Rome then a great famine and pestilence. The people, who always lay the cause of public calamity upon the governors, bruited abroad that Cleander was the cause of the plague and the famine, and therefore should die. Cleander, to stop this rumor and cause the people to hold their peace, had the emperor's horsemen rush through the town and suburbs, slaying and wounding innumerable. But the people began to take houses and fight from the windows so well that the horsemen were constrained to retire. Fadilla, the sister of Commodus, seeing this civil war commenced and raised by Cleander, went to find her brother, whom she found among his harlots. All bewept she fell on her knees before him, saying, "Sir, my brother, you are here taking your pleasures, and know not the things that pass, nor the danger wherein you are. For both yours and our blood is in peril, to be altogether exterminated by the war and civil stir Cleander has raised in the town. He has armed your forces, and has made them rush against the people, and has brought them unto a slaughter more than barbarous, filling the streets with Roman blood. If you do not soon put to death the author of this evil, the people will fall upon you and us, and tear us in pieces." Saying these words, she tore her garments and was very sad, as it were desperate. Many also who were present increased the fear of Commodus by their persuasions; fearing some great danger to himself, he sent in haste for Cleander, who knew nothing of his complaint. As soon as he arrived, Commodus had his head cut off and carried on a pike through the town, and the sight of the head appeased the people.

~

French Academy:

And lastly, for the upshot and perfection of all happiness and felicity in this world, he instructs him how he may lead a quiet and peaceable life in beholding the wonderful works of the divinity, which he is to adore and honor, and in the amendment and correction of his manners naturally corrupted, by squaring them after the pattern of virtue, that so he may be made worthy and fit to govern human affairs, for the profit of many; and at length attain to the perfection of a wise man, by joining together the active life with the contemplative in the certain hope and expectation of a second, immortal and most blessed life.

Anti-Machiavel:

Very true it is, that among Christians there must be some contemplatives, that is to say, studious people who give themselves to holy letters in order to teach others. But we do not find by the documents of that religion that there is allowed any idle contemplation of dreamers, who do nothing but imagine dreams and toys in their brains; but a contemplative life of laboring studious people is only approved, who give themselves to letters to teach others. For after they have accomplished their studies, they ought to put in use and action that which they know, bringing into an active life that which they have learned by their study in their contemplative life. And those who use this otherwise do not follow the precepts of the true Christian religion.

~

French Academy:

For this cause the ancient Romans built two temples joined together, the one being dedicated to virtue and the other to honor; but yet in such sort that no man could enter into that of honor except first he passed through the other of virtue.

Anatomie of the Minde:

Marcellus building a temple, which he called the temple of Honor, did so place and situate the same, as none could have entrance thereunto, except first he came through Virtue's temple. Signifying thereby, that the way to honor, is by virtue only, not by favor, money, nor other means.

VINDICIAE,
CONTRA TY-
RANNOS:

SIVE,

DE PRINCIPIS IN Populum, Populique in Principem, legitima potestate,

STEPHANO IVNIO
Bruto Celta, Auctore.

EDIMBVRGI, AN-
NO M. D. LXXIX.

4. *Vindiciae contra tyrannos*

The Huguenot tract on the right of resistance, *Vindiciae contra tyrannos* (translated as *A defense of liberty against tyrants*, 1579), was published in Basel with a false imprint of Edinburgh, under the pseudonym Stephanus Brutus Junius—alluding to both Marcus Junius Brutus (of *Julius Caesar*) and Lucius Junius Brutus, who deposed Tarquin and established the Roman Republic (*The Rape of Lucrece*). Machiavelli advised that "whoever takes up a tyranny and does not kill Brutus, and whoever makes a free state and does not kill the sons of Brutus, maintains himself for little time." The *Vindiciae*'s account of Tarquin reads:

> Tarquinius Superbus was therefore esteemed a tyrant, because being chosen neither by the people nor the senate, he intruded himself into the kingdom only by force and usurpation . . . The true causes why Tarquinius was deposed, were because he altered the custom, whereby the king was obliged to advise with the senate on all weighty affairs; that he made war and peace according to his own fancy; that he treated confederacies without demanding counsel and consent from the people or senate; that he violated the laws whereof he was made guardian; briefly that he made no reckoning to observe the contracts agreed between the former kings, and the nobility and people of Rome

Anti-Machiavel:

> Tarquin, who enterprised to slay his father-in-law king Servius Tullius to obtain the kingdom of Rome, showed well by that act and many others that he was a very tyrant. . . when he changed his just and royal domination into a tyrannical government, he became a contemner and despiser of all his subjects, both plebian and patrician. He brought a confusion and a corruption into justice; he took a greater number of servants into his guard than his predecessors had; he took away the authority from the Senate; moreover, he dispatched criminal and civil cases after his fancy, and not according to right; he cruelly punished those who complained of that change of estate as conspirators against him; he caused many great and notable persons to die secretly without any form of justice; he imposed tributes upon the people against the ancient form, to the impoverishment and oppression of some more than others; he had spies to discover what was said of him, and punished rigorously those who blamed either him or his government

The introduction to *The Rape of Lucrece* echoes these passages, and may reflect what T.S. Eliot called Shakespeare's "shameless lifting" from *Anti-Machiavel*:

> Tarquinius, for his excessive pride surnamed Superbus, after he had caused his own father-in-law Servius Tullius to be cruelly murdered, and, contrary to the Roman laws and customs, not requiring or staying for the people's suffrages, had possessed himself of the kingdom . . . the people were so moved, that with one consent and a general acclamation the Tarquins were all exiled, and the state government changed from kings to consuls

The *Vindiciae*'s preface, which has been ascribed to the author of *Anti-Machiavel*,[30] includes an edict of Theodosius II and Valentinian III, whereby emperors became subject to Roman law; the edict is also transcribed in full in *Anti-Machiavel*. The *Vindiciae*'s preface challenged "the Machiavellians are free to descend into the arena: let them come forth. As we have said, we shall use the true and legitimate weapons of Holy Scripture"[31] *Anti-Machiavel*, on the other hand, "must fight against their impiety . . . not by assailing them with the arms of the holy Scripture . . . but by their proper arms and weapons" (that is, pagan authors). *Anti-Machiavel* and the *Vindiciae* draw from many of the same sources, biblical and classical; this in itself is unsurprising, but the similarities are so extensive as to indicate at the least a strong influence.

The *Vindiciae*'s authorship is still unresolved.[32] It was first attributed to François Hotman, author of the *Francogallia* (1573), another Huguenot "Monarchomach" treatise. Hotman's son Jean had been a tutor in the household of English ambassador Sir Amias Paulet, while Francis Bacon happened to be living there. Theodore Beza, author of *De jure magistratuum* (The Right of Magistrates, 1574), was then thought responsible; his connections with the Bacon family were noted previously. The next candidate was Philippe du Plessis Mornay, a Huguenot author and diplomat who fled to England after the St. Bartholomew's Day massacres. During the peace negotiations at Poitiers in late 1577, Bacon met Mornay, who later invited Anthony Bacon to

---

[30] By Mastellone (1969); see Victoria Kahn, "Reading Machiavelli: Innocent Gentillet's Discourse on Method." *Political Theory* 22, no. 4 (1994): 539-60.
[31] *Vindiciae, contra tyrannos*, tr. George Garnett, p. 11. Cambridge: Cambridge University Press, 1994. Other citations are from the 1648 English translation dubiously attributed to William Walker, supposed executioner of Charles I.
[32] Barker, Ernest. "The Authorship of the *Vindiciae Contra Tyrannos*." *Cambridge Historical Journal* 3, no. 2 (1930): 164-81. Also Garnett, ibid. pp. lv—lxxvi.

Montauban, and the two became good friends.[33] Finally Hubert Languet, or a collaboration between Languet and Mornay, was credited with the *Vindiciae*. Languet corresponded extensively with Sir Philip Sidney, a friend of Bacon's. Bacon himself has not been proposed as a possible author of the *Vindiciae*, but it is interesting to note that he had connections to all candidates, a fact that has so far been overlooked.

Parallelisms

Vindiciae contra tyrannos:

Notwithstanding, the Machiavellians are free to descend into the arena: let them come forth. As we have said, we shall use the true and legitimate weapons of Holy Scripture, of the philosophy of ethics and of the laws of the commonwealth, of customs of nations, and of historical examples; then we shall boldly join battle with them on foot

Anti-Machiavel:

I see well it is to no purpose to cite reasons against this atheist and his disciples, who believe neither God nor religion; wherefore, before I pass any further, I must fight against their impiety, and make it appear to their eyes, if they have any, not by assailing them with the arms of the holy Scripture—for they do not merit to be so assailed, and I fear to pollute the holy Scriptures among people so profane and defiled with impiety—but by their proper arms and weapons, whereby their ignorance and beastliness defends their renewed atheism

∼

Vindiciae contra tyrannos:

As for the characteristics of the method of teaching (I address myself to philosophers and disputants): from the effects and consequences he inferred the causes and major propositions or rules, in order to demonstrate the matter more clearly and definitively. He rendered it visible and comprehensible, as if ascending through certain degrees to the peak: so that in the manner of geometricians—whom he seems to

---

[33] See Daphne du Maurier, *Golden Lads* (1975).

have wanted to imitate in this matter—from a point he draws a line, from the line a plane, and from the plane he constitutes a solid

Anti-Machiavel:

Aristotle and other philosophers teach us, and experience confirms, that there are two ways to come unto the knowledge of things. The one, when from the causes and maxims, men come to knowledge of the effects and consequences. The other, when contrary, by the effects and consequences we come to know the causes and maxims… The first of these ways is proper and peculiar unto the mathematicians, who teach the truth of their theorems and problems by their demonstrations drawn from maxims, which are common sentences allowed of themselves for true by the common sense and judgment of all men

～

Vindiciae contra tyrannos:

In treating these questions we will bear in mind this old and, to be sure, perfect image of the governance of kingdoms, as a legitimate, chaste, and blameless matron without any excessive adornment; in its place these Machiavellians do not hesitate to present us with an illegitimate, painted, lewd, and wanton harlot. This ancient method of administering provinces, kingdoms, and empires was that of your ancestors; and princes who were well endowed with every sort of royal virtue carefully kept to it for as long as they lived, as something passed on from hand to hand

Anti-Machiavel:

And we need not be abashed if those of Machiavelli's nation, who hold the principal estates in the government of France, have forsaken the ancient manner of our French ancestors' government, to bring France into use with a new form of managing and ruling their country, taught by Machiavelli

～

Vindiciae contra tyrannos:

And clearly, in order that this majesty of the king and the ancient rights of the peoples should be restored in their entirety amongst the Gauls, some of your own compatriots have, as generals, led armies against that nation which, despising both God and man and buoyed up by the strengths and artifices of cunning and perfidy, wholly concentrated its talent, power, and force on reducing the Gauls—who are free by nature and entirely autonomous in their way of life and the laws and practices of antiquity—to a servitude of barbarous cruelty

Anti-Machiavel:

The French were reputed to be frank and liberal, far from all servitude; but now our stupidity, carelessness, and cowardice make us servants and slaves to the most dastardly and cowardly nation of Christendom... Let us then stir up in ourselves the generosity and virtue of our valiant great grandfathers, and show that we are come from the race of those good and noble Frenchmen, our ancestors, who in time past have brought under their subjection so many foreign nations, and who so many times have vanquished the Italian race, who would make us now serve

~

Vindiciae contra tyrannos:

A tyrant subverts the state, pillages the people, lays stratagems to entrap their lives, breaks promise with all, scoffs at the sacred obligations of a solemn oath, and therefore is he so much more vile than the vilest of usual malefactors... Therefore as Bartolus says, "He may either be deposed by those who are lords in sovereignty over him, or else justly punished according to the law Julia, which condemns those who offer violence to the public"

Anti-Machiavel:

All these ten kinds of tyrannical actions set down by Bartolus, are they not so many maxims of Machiavelli's doctrine taught to a prince? Did he not say that a prince ought to take away all virtuous people, lovers of their commonwealth; to maintain partialities and divisions; to impoverish his subjects, to nourish wars, and to do all these things which Bartolus said to be the works of tyrants? We need then no more doubt that the purpose of Machiavelli was to form a true tyrant, and that he has stolen from Bartolus one part of his tyrannical doctrine, which yet he has much augmented and enriched. For he adds that a prince ought to govern himself by his own counsel, and ought not to suffer any to discover unto him the truth of things; and that he ought not to care for any religion, neither observe any faith or oath, but ought to be cruel, a deceiver, a fox in craftiness, greedy, inconstant, unmerciful, and perfectly wicked, if it be possible, as we shall see hereafter

~

Vindiciae contra tyrannos:

Let us then reject these detestable, faithless, and impious vanities of the court-marmosets, which make kings gods, and receive their sayings as oracles

Anti-Machiavel:

And it seems unto me that this name of marmoset is very proper and fit for such people, and that it merits well to be called again back into use. And I believe it is drawn from hence that such people go marmoting, murmuring and whispering secretly in princes' ears flattering speeches

~

Vindiciae contra tyrannos:

It may be the flatterers of the court will reply, that God has resigned his power unto kings, reserving heaven for himself, and allowing the earth to them to reign, and govern there according to their own fancies; briefly that the great ones of the world hold a divided empire with God himself… This discourse, I say, is worthy of the execrable Domitian who (as Suetonius recites) would be called God and Lord. But altogether unworthy of the ears of a Christian prince, and of the mouth of good subjects, that sentence of God Almighty must always remain irrevocably true, "I will not give My glory to any other," that is, no man shall have such absolute authority, but I will always remain Sovereign

Anti-Machiavel:

The first point then, which is that the absolute power of a prince does not stretch above God, is a matter confessed by all. And there were never found any princes, or very few, who would soar and mount so high as to enterprise upon that which belonged unto God. Even the emperors Caligula and Domitian are blamed and detested by the pagan histories, which had no true knowledge of God, for that they dared enterprise upon God and that which pertained to him

Vindiciae contra tyrannos:

Seeing then that kings are only the lieutenants of God, established in the Throne of God by the Lord God himself, and the people are the people of God, and that the honour which is done to these lieutenants proceeds from the reverence which is borne to those that sent them to this service, it follows of necessity that kings must be obeyed for God's cause, and not against God, and then, when they serve and obey God, and not other ways

Anti-Machiavel:

We also see by the law of God the same absolute power is given unto kings and sovereign princes, for it is written that they shall have full power over the goods and persons of their subjects. And although God has given them their absolute power, as to his ministers and lieutenants on earth, yet he would not have the use of it but with a temperance and moderation of the second power, which is ruled by reason and equity, which we call civil

Vindiciae contra tyrannos:

The Emperors Theodosius and Valentinian to Volusianus, Great Provost of the Empire.

> It is a thing well becoming the majesty of an emperor, to acknowledge himself bound to obey the laws. Our authority depending on the authority of the laws, and in very deed to submit the principality to law, is a greater thing than to bear rule. We therefore make it known unto all men, by the declaration of this our Edict, that we do not allow ourselves, or repute it lawful, to do anything contrary to this. Dated 11 June at Ravenna, under the consuls Florentius and Dionysius

Anti-Machiavel:

This is that power which all good princes have so practiced—letting their absolute power cease without using any, unless in a demonstration of majesty, to make their estate more venerable and better obeyed—that in all their actions and in all their commands they desire to subject and submit themselves to laws and to reason… And truly all the good

Roman emperors have always held this language and have so practiced their power, as we read in their histories. The emperor Theodosius made an express law for it, which is so good to be marked that I thought it good to translate it word for word.

> It is the majesty of him that governs to confess himself bound to laws, so much does our authority depend upon law. And assuredly it is a far greater thing to the empire itself to submit his empire and power unto laws. And that which we will not be lawful unto us, we show it unto others by the oracle of this our present edict. Given at Ravenna the eleventh day of June, in the year of the consulship of Florentius and Dionysius

~

Vindiciae contra tyrannos:

Now, if they were true friends indeed, they would desire and endeavor that the king might become more powerful, and more assured in his estate according to that notable saying of Theopompus, king of Sparta, after the ephores or controllers of the kingdom were instituted. "The more" (said he) "are appointed by the people to watch over, and look to the affairs of the kingdom, the more those who govern shall have credit, and the more safe and happy the state"

Anti-Machiavel:

We read that the emperor Alexander Severus was very modest, soft, clement, and affable towards his subjects, wherewith Mammaea his mother was not content; so that one day she said unto him that he had made his authority disregarded and contemptible by his clemency. He answered, "Yea, but I have made my estate so much the longer and more assured." …The same notable speech of Alexander is attributed to Theopompus, king of Sparta, who knew that the puissance of a king is good and excellent when kings use it well; but because there were far more kings who abused their powers, he provided for himself and his successors certain censors and correctors, which were called Ephori. Some said to Theopompus that by this establishment of Ephori he had lessened and enfeebled his power; "Nay then," he said, "I have fortified it and made it perdurable." Meaning to say, as true it is, that there is nothing which better fortifies nor which makes more firm and stable a prince's estate, than when he governs himself with such a sweet moderation that he even submits himself to the observation of laws and censures

~

Vindiciae contra tyrannos:

But we see in many places, that when the people has despised the law, or made covenants with Baal, God has delivered them into the hands of Eglon, Jabin, and other kings of the Canaanites. And as it is one and the same covenant, so those who do break it, receive like punishment... Thou hast neglected the Lord thy God, He also has rejected thee, that thou reign no more over Israel. This has been so certainly observed by the Lord, that the very children of Saul were deprived of their paternal inheritance, for that he, having committed high treason, did thereby incur the punishment of tyrants, which affect a kingdom that in no way pertains to them. And not only the kings, but also their children and successors, have been deprived of the kingdom by reason of such felony. Solomon revolted from God to worship idols. Incontinently the prophet Ahijah foretells that the kingdom shall be divided under his son Rehoboam

Anti-Machiavel:

David was marvelously happy in war, and always victorious over his enemies, because he was a good prince, fearing God and honoring his holy religion. Solomon his son, as long as he served God sincerely without feigning and hypocrisy, prospered very well and marvelously in a great and happy peace, and none dared stir him. But as soon as he began to practice the doctrine which Machiavelli teaches, namely to have a feigned and dissembled religion and devotion, straight had he enemies on his head, who rose up against him; as Hadad the Edomite, and Razin, who made war upon him. So generally may be said of all the kings of Judah and Israel, one after another; that God has always prospered those who were pure and sincere in religion, and who have had his service in recommendation; and contrary, upon those impure and hypocrites in religion he has heaped ruins, calamities, and other vengeances

~

Vindiciae contra tyrannos:

Ahab, king of Israel, could not compel Naboth to sell him his vineyard; but rather if he had been willing, the law of God would not permit it

Anti-Machiavel:

For God would not that princes use their absolute power so far as to constrain their subjects to sell their goods, as is declared to us in the example of Naboth… And hereunto agrees the divine right, whereby it is showed to us that king Ahab ought not to take away the vineyard from Naboth his subject

~

Vindiciae contra tyrannos:

The queen Athalia, after the death of her son Ahaziah king of Judah, put to death all those of the royal blood, except little Joas, who, being yet in the cradle, was preserved by the piety and wisdom of his aunt Jehoshabeah. Athalia possesses herself of the government, and reigned six years over Judah… Finally, Jehoiada, the high priest, the husband of Jehoshabeah, having secretly made a league and combination with the chief men of the kingdom, did anoint and crown king his nephew Joas, being but seven years old. And he did not content himself to drive the Queen Mother from the royal throne, but he also put her to death, and presently overthrew the idolatry of Baal. This deed of Jehoiada is approved, and by good reason, for he took on him the defence of a good cause, for he assailed the tyranny, and not the kingdom

Anti-Machiavel:

King Ahaziah of Judah was the son of a foreign woman named Athalia, daughter of the king of Samaria. This king governed himself by Samaritans, who were much hated by the people of Judah. At the persuasion of his mother, he gave them the principal charges and offices of his kingdom, despising and casting aside the wisest and most virtuous of his kingdom, by whom he should have governed, after the example of his predecessors. This was the cause of that king's destruction; for as Jehu was destroying the house of Ahab, he also slew Ahaziah, and exterminated almost all his race, as a partner and friend who maintained Ahab. If Ahaziah had governed himself by people of his own kingdom rather than by strangers, that evil hap would not have come to him

~

Vindiciae contra tyrannos:

For the wisdom of a senate, the integrity of a judge, the valour of a captain, may peradventure enable a weak prince to govern well

Anti-Machiavel:

Contrarily, if the prince be not wise at all—for it is not incompatible nor inconvenient to be a prince and to be unwise withal—yet having this resolution to govern himself by counsel, his affairs will carry themselves better than being governed by the head

~

Vindiciae contra tyrannos:

There is, therefore, both truly mildness in putting to death some, and as certainly cruelty in pardoning of others

Anti-Machiavel:

For a prince ought well to consider when, how, to whom, and why he pardons a fault, because it is not clemency but cruelty when a prince may do justice and does it not, as Saint Louis said

~

Vindiciae contra tyrannos:

If the prince has committed some crime, as adultery, parricide, or some other wickedness, behold amongst the heathen, the learned lawyer Papinian who will reprove Caracalla to his face, and had rather die than obey, when his cruel prince commands him to lie and palliate his offence; nay, although he threaten him with a terrible death, yet would he not bear false witness

Anti-Machiavel:

For briefly, a prince may well give laws unto his subjects, but it must not be contrary to nature and natural reason. This was the cause why the great lawyer Papinian, who understood both natural and civil law, loved better to die than to obey Caracalla, who had commanded him to excuse before the Senate his parricide, committed in the person of Geta his brother. For Papinian, knowing that such a crime was against natural right, would not have obeyed the emperor if he had commanded him to perpetrate it, nor would obey him so far therein as to excuse it

Bassianus [Caracalla], not ignorant that the Senate would find this murder very strange, desired that great lawyer Papinian, his kinsman and Chancellor under Severus, to go to the Senate and make his excuses by an oration well set out: That he had done well to slay his brother, and that he had reason and occasion to do it. Papinian, who was a good man, answered that it was not so easy to excuse a parricide as it was to commit it. Bassianus, grieved at this refusal, had one of his attendants straight cut off his head

~

Vindiciae contra tyrannos:

And instead of approving that which that villainous woman said to Caracalla, that whatsoever he desired was allowed him, we will maintain that nothing is lawful but what the law permits. And absolutely rejecting that detestable opinion of the same Caracalla, that princes give laws to others, but received none from any; we will say, that in all kingdoms well established, the king receives the laws from the people; the which he ought carefully to consider and maintain; and whatsoever, either by force or fraud he does, in prejudice of them, must always be reputed unjust

Anti-Machiavel:

We read likewise that Caracalla, beholding one day his mother-in-law Julia with an eye of incestuous concupiscence, she said unto him, "If thou wilt, thou mayst; knowest thou not that it belongs unto thee to give the law, not to receive it?" Which talk so enflamed him yet more with lust that he took her to wife in marriage. Hereupon historiographers note that if Caracalla had known well what it was to give a law, he would have detested and prohibited such incestuous and abominable copulations, and not to have authorized them

~

Vindiciae contra tyrannos:

Julian the apostate, did cast off Christ Jesus to cleave unto the impiety and idolatry of the pagans: but within a small time after he fell to his confusion through the force of the arm of Christ, whom in mockery he called the Galilean

Anti-Machiavel:

The emperor Julian, who was called the Apostate, all the time of his youth, in the time of his uncle Constantine the Great, was instructed in the Christian religion; but upon a foolish curiosity he gave himself to diviners and sorcerers, to know things to come, which made him forsake Christianity... Finally after he had reigned for the space of a year and seven months, he was slain at the age of thirty-two years, making war against the Persians. Some write that as he died he blasphemed spitefully against Christ, crying "Thou hast vanquished, thou Galilean"

∼

Vindiciae contra tyrannos:

Tarquinius Superbus was therefore esteemed a tyrant, because being chosen neither by the people nor the senate, he intruded himself into the kingdom only by force and usurpation

The true causes why Tarquinius was deposed, were because he altered the custom, whereby the king was obliged to advise with the senate on all weighty affairs; that he made war and peace according to his own fancy; that he treated confederacies without demanding counsel and consent from the people or senate; that he violated the laws whereof he was made guardian; briefly that he made no reckoning to observe the contracts agreed between the former kings, and the nobility and people of Rome

Anti-Machiavel:

Tarquin, who enterprised to slay his father-in-law king Servius Tullius to obtain the kingdom of Rome, showed well by that act and many others that he was a very tyrant... For they say that when he changed his just and royal domination into a tyrannical government, he became a contemner and despiser of all his subjects, both plebian and patrician. He brought a confusion and a corruption into justice; he took a greater number of servants into his guard than his predecessors had; he took away the authority from the Senate; moreover, he dispatched criminal and civil cases after his fancy, and not according to right; he cruelly punished those who complained of that change of estate as conspirators against him; he caused many great and notable persons to die secretly without any form of justice; he imposed tributes upon the people against the ancient form, to the impoverishment and oppression of some more than others; he had spies to discover what was said of him, and punished rigorously those who blamed either him or his government. These are the colors wherewith the histories paint Tarquin, and these are ordinarily the colors and livery of all tyrants' banners, whereby they may be known

∼

Vindiciae contra tyrannos:

Besides all this, anciently every year, and since less often, to wit, when some urgent necessity required it, the general or three estates were assembled, where all the provinces and towns of any worth, to wit, the burgesses, nobles, and ecclesiastical persons, did all of them send their deputies, and there they did publicly deliberate and conclude of that which concerned the public estate. Always the authority of this assembly was such that what was there determined, whether it were to treat peace, or make war, or create a regent in the kingdom, or impose some new tribute, it was ever held firm and inviolable; nay, which is more by the authority of this assembly, the kings convinced of loose intemperance, or of insufficiency, for so great a charge or tyranny, were disthronized

Anti-Machiavel:

Our kings of old in France used the same course that these good emperors did; for they often convocated the three Estates of the kingdom to have their advice and counsel in affairs of great consequence which touched the interest of the commonwealth. And it is seen by our histories that the general assembly of the Estates was commonly done for three causes. One, when there was a question to provide for the kingdom a governor or regent; as when kings were young, or lost the use of their understanding by some accident, or were captives or prisoners; in these cases the three Estates assembled to obtain a governor for the realm. Again, when there was cause to reform the kingdom, to correct the abuses of officers and magistrates, and to bring things unto their ancient and first institution and integrity. For kings caused the Estates to assemble, because being assembled from all parts of the kingdom, they might better be informed of all abuses and evil behaviors committed therein, and might also better work the means to remedy them; because commonly there is no better physician than he that knows well the disease and the causes thereof. The third cause why there was made an assembly of Estates was when there was a necessary cause to lay a tribute or tax upon the people; for then in a full assembly the representatives were showed the necessity of the king's and the kingdom's affairs, who graciously and courteously entreated the people to aid and help the king but with so much money as they themselves thought to be sufficient and necessary

~

Vindiciae contra tyrannos:

About the year 1300 Pope Boniface VIII, seeking to appropriate to his See the royalties that belonged to the crown of France, Philip the Fair, the then king, did taunt him somewhat sharply: the tenor of whose tart letters are these:

> "Philip by the Grace of God, King of the French, to Boniface, calling himself Sovereign Bishop, little or no health at all. Be it known to the great foolishness and unbounded rashness, that in temporal matters we have only God for our superior, and that the vacancy of certain churches belongs to us by royal prerogative, and that appertains to us only to gather the fruits, and we will defend the possession thereof against all opposers with the edge of our swords, accounting them fools, and without brains who hold a contrary opinion."

In those times all men acknowledged the pope for God's vicar on earth, and head of the universal church. Insomuch, that (as it is said) common error went instead of a law, notwithstanding the Sorbonists being assembled, and demanded, made answer, that the king and the kingdom might safely, without blame or danger of schism, exempt themselves from his obedience, and flatly refuse that which the pope demanded; for so much as it is not the separation but the cause which makes the schism, and if there were schism, it should be only in separating from Boniface, and not from the church, nor the pope, and that there was no danger nor offence in so remaining until some honest man were chosen pope

Anti-Machiavel:

Yet we read in our histories that our kings of France have many times hindered popes from drawing silver out of the realm, by annates, tenths, bulls, and other means; as in the time of Boniface VIII, Benedict XI, Julius II and III. But concerning this matter it is good to mark the determination made in 1410 by our masters of the faculty of the Sorbonne, and by all the University of Paris; who resolved in a general congregation that the French church was not bound to pay any silver to the pope in any manner whatsoever, unless by the way of a charitable subsidy

As in the time of king Philip IV, Pope Boniface VIII made a decretal whereby he generally forbade all emperors, kings, and princes of Christendom to levy any tribute upon the clergy, upon pain of a present excommunication, without any other commissance or declaration. The king, because this was against his privileges (by the advice of his council, the prelates of his country, and the faculty of theology of Paris), appealed from the pope, as inferior, to the first future council, as superior

Likewise, the pope Boniface, of whom we have spoken before, was declared a heretic by the said University and faculty of theology; not that he erred in the faith (for it was a thing whereof he had little care), but because he would needs enterprise upon the king's privileges. But as soon as he was declared a heretic, all the kingdom of France retired from his obedience

EL INGENIOSO
HIDALGO DON QVI-
XOTE DE LA MANCHA,

Compueſto por Miguel de Ceruantes Saauedra.

DIRIGIDO AL DVQVE DE BEIAR,
Marques de Gibraleon, Conde de Benalcaçar, y Baña-
res, Vizconde de la Puebla de Alcozer, Señor de
las villas de Capilla, Curiel, y
Burguillos

Año, 1605.

CON PRIVILEGIO,
EN MADRID Por Iuan de la Cueſta.

Vendeſe en caſa de Franciſco de Robles, librero del Rey nro ſeñor

First edition (1605) *Don Quixote* with "BACON" acrostic left-center

5. *Don Quixote*

> With its preposterous inns full of belated characters from Italian storybooks and its preposterous mountains teeming with lovelorn poetasters disguised as Arcadian shepherds, the picture Cervantes paints of the country is about as true and typical of seventeenth-century Spain as Santa Claus is true and typical of the twentieth-century North Pole. Indeed, Cervantes seems to know Spain as little as Gogol did central Russia . . . throughout these adventures there is a mass of monstrous inaccuracies at every step. The author avoids descriptions that would be particular and might be verified. It is quite impossible to follow these rambles in central Spain across four of six provinces, in the course of which until we reach Barcelona in the northeast one does not meet with a single known town or cross a single river. Cervantes's ignorance of places is wholesale and absolute, even in respect of Argamasilla in the La Mancha district, which some consider the more or less definite starting point.
>
> Vladimir Nabokov, *Lectures on Don Quixote*

In the prologue to his masterpiece, Cervantes says he is "in show a father, yet in truth but a step-father to Don Quixote"; over the course of the novel's two parts, he repeats more than forty times that the true author is Arabian historian Cid Hamet Ben Engeli. No such writer exists, and some have interpreted this as "Lord Hamlet son of England." In 1613, between the two parts of *Quixote*, Cervantes published his *Novelas emplejares* (Exemplary Novels), and again in the preface he plays with the idea of authorship, calling himself

> the author of *Galatea*, *Don Quixote de la Mancha*, *The Journey to Parnassus*, which he wrote in imitation of Cesare Caporali Perusino, and other works which are current among the public, and perhaps without the author's name.

Cervantes is not credited with any anonymous or pseudonymous publications, and it is strange that, being poor (as he died), after the first part of *Quixote*, an international success, he should have spent time on this much inferior work *Novelas emplajares*. Indeed, *Quixote* stands in sharp contrast to the other works of Cervantes, which are seldom read and generally acknowledged as failures—some have not even been translated into English. In *Attributing Authorship*, Harold Love summarizes the principles of Saint Jerome (as outlined by Michel Foucault) in determining scriptural canonicity, one of which is "if among several books attributed to an author one is inferior to the others, it must be withdrawn from the list of the author's works."[34] The case of *Quixote* represents the inverse of this rule.

The 1605 first edition of *Quixote*, widely regarded as the most influential novel ever written, went into press immediately following the first (1603) and second (1604) editions of *Hamlet*, widely seen as the world's greatest play (Bacon's *Advancement of Learning* went out in late 1605). By another remarkable coincidence, Shakespeare and Cervantes died just days apart, traditionally on St. George's Day, April 24th, 1616 (England and Spain were on different calendars). Nothing was published in either country to mark their loss—no eulogy, no comment from contemporary writers, not a word is found even in private correspondence. By contrast, Lope de Vega was given a lavish state funeral that lasted several days in 1635.

The case for Bacon's involvement in *DQ* was first made by a barrister and MP, Sir Edwin Durning-Lawrence, whose substantial library (now housed at the University of London) included a 1612 English *DQI* with corrections in what is alleged to be Bacon's handwriting. Durning-Lawrence believed that the English version is really the original, and the Spanish edition published seven years earlier is a translation. Anomalies in translation suggest that this may be the case; for example the title, *El ingenioso hidalgo don Quixote de la Mancha* (The Ingenious Gentleman Don Quixote of the Mancha), is bombastically inflated to *The History of the Valorous and Wittie Knight-Errant Don Quixote of the Mancha*. Several English playwrights, including Ben Jonson and two of Shakespeare's acknowledged collaborators, alluded to or borrowed from *Quixote* long before the 1612 English translation; Francis Beaumont's *Knight of the Burning Pestle* was first performed in 1607. Edward Blount, who published the Shakespeare First Folio, also published the 1612 English edition. Fourteen out of twenty-six Spanish proverbs in Francis Bacon's *Promus* notebook are translated or alluded to in the Shakespeare works. The meaningless proverb "many think there is bacon, and there is only stakes" is repeated five times in *Quixote*.

---

[34] Love, Harold. *Attributing Authorship* p. 18. Cambridge: Cambridge University Press, 2002.

A number of parallels between *Quixote* and the works of Francis Bacon have not been remarked previously, so far as I can determine. Cervantes wrote

la Epica tambien puede escrebirse en prosa, como en verso

epics can also be written in prose, as in verse

Bacon's *Advancement of Learning*:

feigned history... may be styled as well in prose as in verse

~

DQ:

art goes not beyond nature, but only perfects it; so that nature and art mixed together, and art with nature, make an excellent poet

De Augmentis Scientiarum:

[Poetry] is not art, but abuse of art, when instead of perfecting nature it perverts her

~

DQ:

It is one thing to write like a poet, and another like an historian: the poet may say or sing things not as they were, but as they ought to have been; and the historian must write things, not as they ought to be, but as they have been, without adding or taking away aught from the truth

De Augmentis:

[Narrative poetry] raises the mind and carries it aloft, accommodating the shows of things to the desires of the mind, not (like reason and history) buckling and bowing down the mind to the nature of things

Bacon's *Wisdom of the Ancients* (1609), discussing Icarus, Scylla and Charybdis, alludes to Bacon's heraldic motto *mediocria firma*, "the middle way is firm":

the path of virtue lies straight between excess on the one side, and defect on the other. And no wonder that excess should prove the bane of Icarus, exulting in juvenile strength and vigour; for excess is the natural vice of youth, as defect is that of old age; and if a man must perish by either, Icarus chose the better of the two; for all defects are justly esteemed more depraved than excesses. There is some magnanimity in excess, that, like a bird, claims kindred with the heavens; but defect is a reptile, that basely crawls upon the earth

DQ:

> valour is a virtue betwixt two vicious extremes, as cowardice and rashness; but it is less dangerous for him that is valiant to rise to a point of rashness than to fall or touch upon the coward. For, as it is more easy for a prodigal man to be liberal than a covetous, so it is easier for a rash man to be truly valiant than a coward to come to true valour . . . for it sounds better in the hearer's ears, "Such a knight is rash and hardy," than "Such a knight is fearful and cowardly." "I say, signior," answered Don Diego . . . if the statutes and ordinances of knight-errantry were lost, they might be found again in your breast, as in their own storehouse and register."

(This has another parallel in *The Advancement of Learning*: "certain critics are used to say hyperbolically, that if all sciences were lost, they might be found in Virgil.") *The Anatomie of the Minde*:

> Aristotle said [virtuc] is a choosing habit of the mind consisting in a mean between two extremes, of which one exceeds, the other wants much; as Fortitude when it exceeds, falls into rashness, when it faints, into childish fearfulness; and Liberality, when it lavishes out of reason, is called prodigality, when it is not extended any whit, purchases the name of covetousness.

The French Academy:

> We, therefore, holding the mean between these two contrary opinions (as the perfection and goodness of all things consists in mediocrity)

> as illiberality and greed is damnable and no way beseeming a prince, so also is profusion and prodigality; but most praiseworthy it is that he hold a course between both, and that he be liberal . . . But to show how liberality ought to be exercised in a prince, we will first speak of illiberality and prodigality, its two extremes.

Another overlooked anticipation of *Quixote* is found in Ben Jonson's *Poetaster* (1601):

> *Ovid Sr.* Are these the fruits of all my travail and expenses? Is this the scope and aim of thy studies? Are these the hopeful courses wherewith I have so long flattered my expectation from thee? Verses? Poetry? Ovid, whom I thought to see the pleader [lawyer], become Ovid the play-maker?

Ovid Jr. No, sir.

Ovid Sr. Yes, sir; I hear of a tragedy of yours coming forth for the common players there, call'd *Medea* . . . What? shall I have my son a stager now?

Likewise, *DQ* portrays a father who is upset because his son, instead of studying law, spends all his time studying poetry:

> 'I, Sir Don Quixote,' answered the gentleman, 'have a son, whom if I had not, perhaps you would judge me more happy than I am—not that he is so bad, but because not so good as I would have him. He is about eighteen years of age, six of which he hath spent in Salamanca, learning the tongues, Greek and Latin: and, when I had a purpose that he should fall to other sciences, I found him so besotted with poesy, and that science, if so it may be called, that it is not possible to make him look upon the law, which I would have him study, nor divinity, the queen of all sciences . . . All the day long he spends in his criticisms, whether Homer said well or ill in such a verse of his Iliads, whether Martial were bawdy or no in such an epigram, whether such or such a verse in Virgil ought to be understood this way or that way. Indeed, all his delight is in these aforesaid poets, and in Horace, Persius, Juvenal, and Tibullus

Don Quixote and *Discours politiques et militaires*

Don Quixote's prologue:

> Being one day walking in the exchange of Toledo, a certain boy by chance would have sold divers old quires and scrolls of books to a squire that walked up and down in that place, and I, being addicted to read such scrolls, though I found them torn in the streets, borne away by this my natural inclination, took one of the quires in my hand, and perceived it to be written in Arabical characters, and seeing that although I knew the letters, yet could I not read the substance, I looked about to view whether I could perceive any Moor turned Spaniard thereabouts that could read them; nor was it very difficult to find there such an interpreter . . . He demanded fifty pounds of raisins and three bushels of wheat, and promised to translate them speedily, well, and faithfully. But I, to hasten the matter more, lest I should lose such an unexpected and welcome treasure, brought him to my house, where he translated all the work in less than a month and a half, even in the manner that it is here recounted.

Similarly, Thomas Shelton's 1612 English edition claims to have been translated in a remarkably short time:

> Having translated some five or six years ago, the *History of Don Quixote*, out of the Spanish tongue into English, in the space of forty days—being thereunto more than half enforced through the importunity of a very dear friend that was desirous to understand the subject—after I had given him once a view thereof, I cast it aside, where it lay long time neglected in a corner, and so little regarded by me, as I never once set hand to review or correct the same. Since when, at the entreaty of others my friends, I was content to let it come to light, conditionally that someone or other would peruse and amend the errors escaped, my many affairs hindering me from undergoing that labour…

François de la Noue's *Discours politiques et militaires* (1587, English edition also 1587) has some strong parallels with *Quixote*, and its dedication sounds remarkably similar to Shelton's:

> I chanced to lay my hand upon a heap of papers thrown aside in a corner, as things not regarded, and finding that they deserved to be more diligently gathered together, I began very gladly to read them over; but he would not suffer me, saying they were but scribblings whereon he had employed the most tedious hours of his leisure during his long and straight imprisonment; likewise that among them there was nothing worth the sight, because his continual exercise in warfare wherein he had employed himself had denied him all opportunity to endite well, as also that in these discourses especially (as never meaning other than to pass away the time) he had taken no pains with the polishing or filing of them, and that he was determined never to take them in hand again: so as at that instant I could not obtain anything of him. But the taste that I had then gotten did so set me on edge that all his denial and despising of them did the more confirm me in my desire, neither did I ever ease until by sundry means I had gotten sometime one and sometime another, so long till at length I had gathered all this book.
>
> Afterward having more carefully considered of the value of my bootie, accounting it more precious and profitable than to be kept in the bottom of a hutch, I did what I might to persuade the author thereof to publish it; but in the end seeing that he made so small account of the same, that there was no means to obtain his consent, I adventured unawares to him to go through with my enterprise . . . Howbeit, in as much as it may so fall out that the author, considering what small account he made of his writings, in lieu of rejoicing in the commendations that hereby shall redound unto him, may find fault that I have thus published them of mine own head, and withal that I have thereunto set his name.

The *Discours politiques et militaires* was purportedly written while François de la Noue was in prison at Limburg (Cervantes says *Quixote* was engendered in prison); the sixth discourse consists of a lengthy attack on "the books of Amadis de Gaul and such like," anticipating *DQ*. *DQ* prologue:

> thy labor doth aim at no more than to diminish the authority and acceptance that books of chivalry have in the world. . . let thy project be to overthrow the ill-compiled machina and bulk of those knightly books, abhorred by many, but applauded by more; for, if thou bring this to pass, thou hast not achieved a small matter.

In chapter 47 the canon expands on this:

> those books which are instituted of chivalry or knighthood are very prejudicial to well-governed commonwealths; and although, borne away by an idle and curious desire, I have read the beginning of almost as many as are imprinted of that subject, yet could I never endure myself to finish and read any one of them through; for methinks that somewhat, more or less, they all import one thing, and this hath no more than that, nor the other more than his fellow. And in mine opinion, this kind of writing and invention falls within the compass of the fables called *Milesiae*, which are wandering and idle tales, whose only scope is delight, and not instruction; quite contrary to the project of those called *Fabulae Apologae*, which delight and instruct together.

The sixth discourse of de Noue, treating books of chivalry, also alludes to *Anti-Machiavel* ("the author whereof I know not"):

> That the reading of the books of Amadis de Gaul, & such like is no less hurtful to youth, than the works of Machiavel to age.

> I have heretofore greatly delighted in reading Machiavel's *Discourses* & his *Prince*, because in that same he intreats of high & goodly politic & martial affairs, which many Gentlemen are desirous to learn, as matters meet for their professions. And I must needs confess that so long as I was content slightly to run them over, I was blinded with the gloss of his reasons. But after I did with more ripe judgement thoroughly examine them, I found under that fair show many hidden errors, leading those that walk in them into paths of dishonour and damage. But if any man doubt of my sayings, I would wish him to read a book entitled *Antimachiavellus*, the author whereof I know not, and there shall he see that I am not altogether deceived. Neither do I think greatly to deceive myself, though I also affirm the books of Amadis to be very fit instruments for the corruption of

manners, which I am determined to prove in few words, to the end to dissuade innocent youth from entangling themselves in these invisible snares which are so subtly laid for them.

Parallelisms

Note: Many of these are taken from Francis Carr's *Who Wrote Don Quixote?* (2005) (reproduced here with permission of Philip Carr).

Midsummer Night's Dream (title page, 1619 "False Folio," falsely dated 1600): *Post tenebras lux*: "After darkness, light" (from Job 17:12)

DQ (title page, first edition Spanish 1605): *Post tenebras spero lucem*: "After darkness I hope for light"

~

Merchant of Venice: All that glisters is not gold

DQ: All is not gold that glisters

Bacon, *Promus*: All is not gold that glisters

~

DQ: He that gives quickly, gives twice

Bacon, *Promus*: He who gives quickly, gives twice

~

DQ: Look not a given horse in the mouth

Bacon, *Promus*: To look a given horse in the mouth

~

DQ: Might overcomes right

Bacon, *Promus*: Might overcomes right

Henry IV Part II: O God, that right should overcome this might

~

DQ: The nearer the Church, the further from God

Bacon, *Promus*: The nearer the church, the further from God

Richard III: And thus I clothe my naked villainy, and seem a saint when most I play the devil

~

DQ: One swallow makes not a summer

Bacon, *Promus*: One swallow maketh no summer

Timon of Athens: The swallow follows not the summer

~

DQ: Everyone is the son of his own works

　　　Every man is the Artificer of his own fortune

Bacon, "Of Fortune":

　But chiefly the mould of a man's fortune is in his own hands

King Lear:

　When we are sick in Fortune—often the surfeit of our own behavior

~

DQ: Statutes not kept are the same as if they were not made

Bacon, Note to Queen Elizabeth: The cessation and abstinence to execute these unnecessary laws do mortify the execution of such as are wholesome

Measure for Measure: In time the rod becomes more mocked than feared

~

DQ: He who does not rise with the sun does not enjoy the day

Bacon, *Promus*: To rise early is very healthy *Diliculo surgere saluberrimum est.*

Twelfth Night: *Diliculo surgere*, thou knowest

~

DQ: God's help is better than early rising

Bacon, *Promus*: It is better to have God's help than to keep getting up early (in Spanish)

∼

DQ: He that is warned is half armed

Bacon, *Promus*: Warned and half armed (Also occurs in Spanish)

∼

DQ: I know where my shoe wrings me

Bacon, *Promus*: Myself can tell best where my shoe wrings me

∼

Merry Wives of Windsor: As good luck would have it (first occurrence)

DQ: As Sancho's ill luck would have it

∼

DQ: Without a wink of sleep

Cymbeline: I have not slept one wink (first occurrence)

∼

DQ: What put you in this pickle?

The Tempest: How cam'st thou in this pickle?

∼

Twelfth Night: If you desire the spleen, and will laugh yourself into stitches, follow me. (first occurrence, "in stitches")

DQ: Ready to split his sides with laughing

∼

DQ: Ill luck seldom comes alone

Hamlet: When sorrows come, they come not single spies, but in battalions

DQ: You are as like the Knight I conquered, as one egg is to another

> The Devil take me (thought Sancho to himself at this instant) if this Master of mine be not a Divine; or if not, as like one as one egg is to another

Winter's Tale: We are almost as like as eggs

~

DQ: Sweet meat must have sour sauce

Shakespeare, Sonnet 118:   Being full of your nere cloying sweetness
                            To bitter sauces did I frame my feeding

~

DQ: Time out of mind

Romeo and Juliet: Time out of mind

~

DQ: I was so free with him as not to mince the matter

Othello: Thy honesty and love doth mince this matter

~

DQ: Walls have ears

Midsummer Night's Dream: No remedy when walls hear without warning

~

DQ: The weakest go to the walls

Romeo and Juliet: The weakest goes to the wall

~

DQ: Murder will out

Hamlet: Murder will speak

~

1 Henry VI, 3 Henry VI: God and Saint George!

DQ: God and Saint George!

~

DQ: comparisons are odious

Much Ado About Nothing: Comparisons are odorous: palabras, neighbor Verges. (palabras = Spanish, words)

~

DQ: A good name is better than riches

Othello: He that filches from me my good name robs me of that which not enriches him and makes me poor indeed

~

DQ: It is such, as is able to make marble relent.

Venus and Adonis: For stone at rain relenteth.

~

DQ: They can expect nothing but their labour for their pains

Troilus and Cressida: I had my labour for my travail

~

Hamlet: anything so overdone is from the purpose of playing, whose end, both at the first and now, was and is to hold, as 'twere, the mirror up to nature

DQ: Seeing the comedy, as Tully affirms, ought to be a mirror of man's life, a pattern of manners, and an image of truth

~

DQ: Dulcinea of Tobosa, the subject on which the extremitie of all commendations my rightly be conferred, how hyperbolicall soever it may be

Bacon, "Of Love": The speaking in a perpetual hyperbole is comely in nothing but in love

~

DQ: An untruth is so much the more pleasing, by how much nearer it resembles the truth

Bacon, "Of Truth": A mixture of a lie doth ever add pleasure

~

DQ: He's a muddled fool, full of lucid intervals

Bacon, *History of Henry VII*: Lucid intervals and happy pauses

~

DQ: Here my exploits suffer'd a total Eclipse

Bacon, *History of Henry VII*: She hath indeed endured strange eclipse

Shakespeare, Sonnet 107: The mortal moon hath her eclipse endured
                           And the sad augurs mock their own presage

~

DQ:

To speak wittily and write conceits belongs only to good wits: the cunningest part in a play is the fool's, because he must not be a fool that would well counterfeit to seem so.

Twelfth Night:

Fool. Are you not mad indeed? Or do you but counterfeit?

~

DQ:

Hunger is the best sauce in the world

Two Noble Kinsmen:

Your hunger needs no sauce

Macbeth:

> my more-having would be as a sauce
> To make me hunger more

Julius Caesar:

> Rudeness is a sauce to his good wit,
> Which gives men stomach to digest his words
> With greater appetite

~

DQ:

> 'I'll hold a wager,' quoth Sancho, 'the dog-bolt hath made a gallimaufry'

Merry Wives of Windsor:

> He wooes both high and low, both rich and poor,
> Both young and old, one with another, Ford;
> He loves the gallimaufry

Winter's Tale:

> Master, there is three carters, three shepherds,
> three neat-herds, three swine-herds, that have made
> themselves all men of hair, they call themselves
> Saltiers, and they have a dance which the wenches
> say is a gallimaufry of gambols

~

DQ:

the rich man not liberal is but a covetous beggar; for he that possesseth riches is not happy in them, but in the spending them; not only in spending, but in well spending them.

Bacon, *Apophthegms New and Old*:

Mr. Bettenham used to say, that riches were like muck: when it lay upon an heap, it gave a stench, and ill odour; but when it was spread upon the ground, then it was the cause of much fruit.

Bacon, "Of Riches":

Of great riches there is no real use, except it be in the distribution; the rest is but conceit.

~

DQ: if the statues and ordinances of knight errantry were lost, they might be found again in your breast.

Bacon, *Advancement of Learning*: certain critics are used to say hyperbolically, that if all sciences were lost, they might be found in Virgil

~

DQ:

I'll tell you, Sancho, this desire of honour is an itching thing. What dost thou think cast Horatius from the bridge all armed into deep Tiber? What egged Curtius to launch himself into the lake? What made Mutius burn his hand? What forced Caesar against all the soothsayers to pass the Rubicon? And, to give you more modern examples, what was it bored those ships, and left those valorous Spaniards on ground, guided by the most courteous Cortez in the New World? All these and other great and several exploits are, have been, and shall be the works of fame, which mortals desire as a reward and part of the immortality which their famous acts deserve

Bacon, "Of Fame":

Fame is of that force, as there is scarcely any great action, wherein it hath not a great part

6. The Alchemy of Eugenius Philalethes

> In truth, much of Bacon's life was passed in a visionary world, amidst things as strange as any that are described in the Arabian Tales, or in those romances on which the curate and barber of Don Quixote's village performed so cruel an *auto-da-fe*, amidst buildings more sumptuous than the palace of Aladdin, fountains more wonderful than the golden water of Parizade, conveyances more rapid than the hippogryph of Ruggiero, arms more formidable than the lance of Astolfo, remedies more efficacious than the balsam of Fierabras.
>
> Thomas Babington Macaulay, "Lord Bacon"

This portrait of Bacon as "in truth" some kind of daydreaming mystic is rather at odds with the conventional image; what was Macaulay's source, did he read this somewhere? One possibility is that he knew the alchemy tracts published under the pseudonym "Eugenius Philalethes (lover of truth)"; they consist of the following:

1650: *Anthroposophia Theomagica*
Anima Magica Abscondita
Magia Adamica
Coelum Terrae
The Man-Mouse Taken in a Trap (a response to Cambridge Platonist Henry More, who had attacked Philalethes in a pamphlet)

1651: *Lumen de Lumine: Or a New Magical Light*
The Second Wash: Or the Moore scoured once more (another rejoinder to More)

1652: *Aula Lucis, or The House of Light* ("by S.N. a modern speculator")
The Fame and Confession of the Fraternity of R.C. (an English translation of the Rosicrucian manifestos, done by "an unknown hand")

1655: *Euphrates, or The Waters of the East*

Usually attributed to Welsh minister Thomas Vaughan, twin brother of better-known metaphysical poet Henry Vaughan, these texts have many parallels in Bacon and many references to *Quixote* (another writer, Eirenaeus Philalethes, does not figure in this discussion). The supremely confident tone of this author does not seem like the voice of an obscure Welsh clergyman—dismissed from his post for royalist sympathies after less than a year (the Vaughans had served kings for centuries)—however it does resemble a relaxed Francis Bacon. *Aula Lucis*:

> It is my design to make over my reputation to a better age, for in this I would not enjoy it, because I know not any from whom I would receive it.

Bacon, last will:

> For my name and memory, I leave it to men's charitable speeches, to foreign nations, and the next ages.

∼

Aula Lucis:

> future times, wearied with the vanities of the present, will perhaps seek after the truth and gladly entertain it. Thus you will see what readers I have predestined for myself

Bacon, *Valerius Terminus*:

> publishing in a manner whereby it shall not be to the capacity nor taste of all, but shall as it were single out and adopt his reader, is not to be laid aside, both for the avoiding of abuse in the excluded, and the strengthening of affection in the admitted

∼

Aula Lucis:

> I could never affect anything that was barren, for sterility and love are inconsistent. Give me a knowledge that is fertile in performances, for theories without their effects are but nothings in the dress of things

Bacon, *Valerius Terminus*:

> Knowledge that tendeth but to satisfaction is but as a courtesan, which is for pleasure and not for fruit or generation

Bacon, *The Great Instauration*:

> That wisdom which we have derived principally from the Greeks is but like the boyhood of knowledge, and has the characteristic property of boys: it can talk, but it cannot generate; for it is fruitful of controversies but barren of works

Philalethes frequently quotes "the divine Virgil" "who was a great poet but a greater philosopher." Francis Bacon felt the same, citing "the best poet [known] to the memory of man" more than any other author, but usually in a scientific or philosophical context.[35] Bacon wrote "certain critics are used to say hyperbolically, that if all sciences were lost, they might be found in Virgil";[36] *Anti-Machiavel* avers:

> if our youths gave themselves only to Virgil to learn all Latin poetry, it is enough; and that author alone, compared to whom all others are but small rivers, might teach them all the poetry that need be known . . . he who well understands Virgil has no need of others for the understanding of poetry. And in every science it seems to be the best, that men may well employ their time, which is dear and short, to read few books, to make good choice of them, and to understand them well.

This sounds like Bacon's famous aphorism: "Some books are to be tasted, others to be swallowed, and some few to be chewed and digested." Bacon frequently quotes the aphorism of Heraclitus ("the obscure," "the weeping philosopher") "dry light is best soul"; *Aula Lucis*:

> hence it is that I move in the sphere of generation and fall short of that test of Heraclitus: "Dry light is best soul"

Wisdom of the Ancients:

> it was excellently said by Heraclitus, "A dry light makes the best soul"

Novum Organum:

> the human understanding resembles not a dry light, but admits a tincture of the will and passions which generate their own system accordingly

Bacon, "Of Friendship":

> it is in truth of operation upon a man's mind, of like virtue as the alchymists use to attribute to their stone for man's body; that it worketh all contrary effects, but still to the good and benefit of nature. But yet without praying in aid of alchmyists, there is manifest image of this in the ordinary course of nature . . . Heraclitus saith well in one of his enigmas, "Dry light is ever the best." And certain it is, that the light that a man receiveth by counsel

---

[35] Schuler, Robert M. "Francis Bacon and Scientific Poetry." *Transactions of the American Philosophical Society*, vol. 82, no. 2, American Philosophical Society, 1992, pp. i–65,

[36] This locution is also in *Don Quixote*: "if the statutes and ordinances of knight errantry were lost, they might be found again in your breast."

from another, is drier and purer than that which cometh from his own understanding and judgment; which is ever infused and drenched in his affections and customs.

Philalethes habitually alludes to *Don Quixote*; *The Fame and Confession of the Fraternity R.C.*:

> some of you may advise me to an assertion of the Capreols of del Phaebo, or a review of the library of that discreet Gentleman of the Mancha, for in your opinion those Knights and these Brothers are equally invisible

Anima Magica Abscondita:

> neither do I care for anything but that interlude of Perendenga in Michael Cervantes

Coelum Terrae:

> this is an humour much like that of Don Quixote, who knew Dulcinea but never saw her

> these men are no more eagles than Sancho; their fancies are like his flights in the blanket and every way as short of the skies

Second Wash:

> To reply to his frolics, as he calls them, were to bray to an ass, like the Alderman in Cervantes

Aula Lucis:

> I speak this to the university Quixotes . . . These buckle on their logic as proof, but it fares with them as with the famous Don: they mistake a basin for a helmet

> The tutor dedicates to his pupil, and the same pupil versifies in commendation of his tutor? Here was a claw; there was never any so reciprocal: surely Rosinante and Dapple might learn of these two

Anthroposophia Theomagica features a title page echoing that of Bacon's *Novum Organum*, which also quotes Daniel 12:4: "Many shall go to and fro, and knowledge shall be increased." It also echoes Bacon's criticisms of Aristotle while invoking *Quixote*:

> Aristotle is a poet in text; his principles are but fancies, and they stand more on our concessions than his bottom. Hence it is that his followers, notwithstanding the assistance of so many ages, can fetch nothing out of him

but notions . . . their compositions are a mere tympany of terms. It is better than a fight in *Quixote* to observe what duels and digladiations they have about him

Anima Magica Abscondita:

Away then with this Peripatetical Philosophy, this vain babbling, as St Paul justly styles it . . . the spirit of error—which is Aristotle's—produceth naught but a multiplicity of notions . . . His followers refine the old notions but not the old creatures. And verily the mystery of their profession consists only in their terms. If their speculations were exposed to the world in a plain dress, their sense is so empty and shallow there is not any would acknowledge them for philosophers. In some discourses, I confess, they have Nature before them, but they go not the right way to apprehend her. They are still in chase but never overtake their game; for who is he amongst them whose knowledge is so entire and regular that he can justify his positions by practice.

Euphrates again sounds very much like an unrestrained Francis Bacon attacking Aristotle:

I have often wondered that any sober spirits can think Aristotle's philosophy perfect when it consists in mere words without any further effects; for of a truth the falsity and insufficiency of a mere notional knowledge is so apparent that no wise man will assert it . . . did not Aristotle's science—if he had any—arise from particulars, or did it descend immediately from universals? . . . I have learned long ago, not from Aristotle but from Roger Bacon, that generals are of small value, nor fitting to be followed, save by reason of particulars. And this is evident in all practices and professions that conduce anything to the benefit of man

Again, *Euphrates* sounds very much like Bacon:

Before his Fall man was a glorious creature, having received from God immortality and perfect knowledge; but in and after his Fall he exchanged immortality for death and knowledge for ignorance

The distinction of God's two books, nature and scripture, a recurring theme of Bacon's, is also echoed in *Euphrates*:

Surely I am one that thinks very honourably of Nature, and if I avoid such disputes as these it is because I would not offend weak consciences. For there are a people who though they dare not think the majesty of God was diminished in that He made the world, yet they dare think the majesty of His Word is much vilified if it be applied to what He hath made—an opinion truly that caries in it a most dangerous blasphemy, namely, that

> God's Word and God's work should be such different things that the one must needs disgrace the other

Advancement of Learning:

> let no man upon a weak conceit of sobriety or an ill-applied moderation think or maintain that a man can search too far, or be too well studied in the book of God's word, or in the book of God's works, divinity or philosophy; but rather let men endeavour an endless progress or proficience in both; only let men beware that they apply both to charity, and not to swelling; to use, and not to ostentation; and again, that they do not unwisely mingle or confound these learnings together

One passage in *Aula Lucis* has several allusions to Bacon: his title and rumored royal descent ("noble Verulam"); his heraldic motto, *mediocria firma* (the middle way is sure), and his phrase for conveying secret knowledge in text, *traditio lampadis*:

> Had their doctrine been such as the universities profess now their silence indeed had been a virtue; but their positions were not mere noise and notion. They were most deep experimental secrets, and those of infinite use and benefit. Such a tradition then as theirs may wear the style of the noble Verulam and is most justly called a Tradition of the Lamp . . . yet I cannot deny that some of them have rather buried the truth than dressed it. For my own part, I shall observe a middle way, neither too obscure nor too open, but such as may serve posterity and add some splendor to the science itself.

Philalethes aroused the antagonism of Cambridge professor Henry More, who initiated a pamphlet battle that took place in the early 1650s. Among other things, More attacked Philalethes for his lack of deference to Aristotle; *Man-Mouse Taken in a Trap* replied:

> The second project is to be more learned and knowing than Aristotle, that great Light (as thou doest blindly all him) of these European parts for these many hundred years together: and not only so, but to be so far above him that I may be his master, that I may lug him and lash him, as Harry Moore's breech should be lash'd. Pish! here is a project indeed, to do all this is nothing.

A prefatory poem in *Man-Mouse* invokes Bacon:

> Had Bacon liv'd in this unknowing Age,
> And seen Experience laugh'd at on the Stage,
> What Tempests would have risen in his Blood

To side an Art, which Nature hath made Good?
...
Tell me in earnest, dost thou think 'tis fit
To believe all that Aristotle writ?
Though he was blinded, yet experience can
Sever the clouds, and make a clearer man

Surprisingly, Frederic Burnham overlooks these many other allusions to Bacon in the works of Eugenius Philalethes, when he writes of "attempt[s] to implicate Bacon in the Hermetic movement":

> More must have been shocked to discover that a mystic like Vaughan [Eugenius Philalethes] would invoke the sanction of an empiricist like Francis Bacon . . . After all, Bacon's repudiation of illuminism, his distrust of imagination, his aversion to fanciful rhetoric, his rejection of philosophical sects, and his suspicion of theosophy were all precedents for the . . . revolt against enthusiasm. Consequently any attempt to associate Bacon with "magicians, soothsayers, Canters and Rosicrucians" was a gross abuse of the revered author.[37]

In *Valerius Terminus, or The Interpretation of Nature* (written around 1603) Bacon styled his annotator "Hermes Stella"; he later flattered James I as Hermes in a masque, exhorting him to acquire a "fit palace for a philosopher's stone." In 1614 Bacon's friend Isaac Casaubon became famous for proving the *Corpus Hermeticum* dates from the Common Era. In the *Advancement of Learning* Bacon speaks of "enigmatical" writing "to remove the vulgar capacities from being admitted to the secrets of knowledges, and to reserve them to selected auditors, or wits of such sharpness as can pierce the veil." *Of the Interpretation of Nature*:

> the discretion anciently observed . . . of publishing in a manner whereby it shall not be to the capacity nor taste of all, but shall as it were single and adopt his reader, is not to be laid aside, both for the avoiding of abuse in the excluded, and the strengthening of affection in the admitted.

Bacon's remarks on alchemy are equivocal; *Wisdom of the Ancients*:

> All that we can say concerning that spring of gold is hardly able to defend us from the violence of the Chymists, if in this regard they set upon us, seeing they promise by that their elixir to effect golden mountains and the restoring of natural bodies, as it were, from the portal of hell. But

---

[37] Burnham, Frederic B. "The More-Vaughan Controversy: The Revolt Against Philosophical Enthusiasm." *Journal of the History of Ideas*, vol. 35, no. 1, 1974, pp. 33–49.

concerning chemistry, and those perpetual suitors for that philosophical elixir, we know, certainly, that their theory is without grounds, and we suspect that their practice also is without certain reward. And therefore, omitting these, of this last part of the parable this is my opinion. I am induced to believe by many figures of the ancients that the conservation and restoration of natural bodies in some sort was not esteemed by them as a thing impossible to be attained, but as a thing abstruse and full of difficulties; and so they seem to intimate in this place, when they report that this one only sprig was found among infinite other trees in a huge and thick wood, which they feigned to be of gold, because gold is the badge of perpetuity, and to be artificially, as it were, inserted, because this effect is to be rather hoped for from art than from any medicine, or simple or natural means.

They report this one only sprig was found among infinite other trees in a huge and thick wood, which they feigned to be of gold, because gold is the badge of perpetuity, and to be artificially as it were inserted, because this effect is to be rather hoped for from Art, than from any Medicine, or simple, or natural means.

Novum Organum:

We ought to make a collection or particular history of all monsters and prodigious births or productions; and, in a word, of everything new, rare, and extraordinary in nature. But this must be done with the most severe scrutiny, lest we depart from truth. Above all, every relation must be considered as suspicious which depends in any degree upon religion, as the prodigies of Livy: and no less so everything that is to be found in the writers on natural magic or alchemy, or such authors who seem all of them to have an unconquerable appetite for falsehood and fable.

This is actually an elaborate allusion to *Gargantua and Pantagruel*:

I find by the ancient Historiographers and Poets, that divers have been born in this world after very strange manners, which would be too long to repeat; read therefore the seventh chapter of Pliny, if you have so much leisure: yet have you never heard of any so wonderful as that of Pantagurel . . . I pass by here the relation of how at every one of his meals he supped the milk of four thousand and six hundred Cows.

The parallels are labored: compare "particular history" and "Historiographers"; "prodigious births" and "born in this world after very strange manners"; "prodigies of Livy" and "seventh chapter of Pliny"; "unconquerable appetite" and "supped the milk of four thousand six hundred Cows." It seems as though Bacon is taking pains to alert us to

Gargantua in relation to alchemy; it abounds with alchemical language and Rabelais introduces himself as the "abstractor of the quintessence." The fifth book, whose authorship is uncertain, has a passage strongly suggestive of Bacon's reform of philosophy:

> 'tis the Novelty of the Experiment, which makes Impressions of their conceptive, cogitative Faculties ... Be Spectators and Auditors of every particular Phaenomenon, and every individual Proposition, within the extent of my Mansion, satiate your selves with all that can fall here under the Consideration of your Visual and Ausculating Powers, and thus emancipate yourselves from the Servitude of Crassous Ignorance.

Rabelais was somewhat scandalous; *Anti-Machiavel* calls him "Satan, being a disguised person amongst the French, in the likeness of a merry jester"; and Bacon would not have wanted to be associated with him; but he was not the only one to make covert references to *Gargantua*. In *The Staple of News* (1625) Ben Jonson alludes to Rabelais' rather vulgar joke about "drawing farts out of a dead ass":

> The art of drawing farts out of dead bodies
> Is by the Brotherhood of the Rosy Cross
> Produced unto perfection in so sweet
> And rich a tincture

The famous *Chymical Wedding of Christian Rosenkreutz* (Strasbourg, 1616), attributed by some to Bacon, contains a passage suggestive of the "four spiritual ways" scheme, which was probably of Hindu or Indian origin:

> By us doth the Bridegroom offer thee a choice between four ways, all of which, if thou dost not sink down in the way, can bring thee to his royal court. The first [fakir, physical] is short but dangerous, and one which will lead thee into rocky places, through which it will be scarcely possible to pass. The second [heart, *bhakti yoga*] is longer, and takes thee circuitously; it is plain and easy, if by the help of the Magnet, thou turnest neither to left nor right. The third [knowledge, *jnana yoga*] is that truly royal way which through various pleasures and pageants of our King, affords thee a joyful journey; but this so far has scarcely been allotted to one in a thousand. By the fourth shall no man reach the place, because it is a consuming way [i.e., by fire], practicable only for incorruptible bodies.

Benedictus Figulus, *Pandora magnalium naturalium aurea et benedicta de Paracelse* (Strasbourg, 1608) also attacks Aristotle, again sounding very much like a relaxed Bacon:

> When reviewing the whole course of my studies, from my youth up, I find—and have indeed hitherto found in my work, and clearly experienced more and more with the lapse of time, as daily experience shows is wont to happen to the true believer and right naturalist—that there are three kinds of Philosophy or Wisdom, of which the world partly makes use, some more than others, some of this and others of that . . . the First is the Common Philosophy of Aristotle, of Plato, and of our own time, which is but a Cagastrian Philosophy, Speculation, and Phantasy, with which, even at the present day, all the Schools are filled, and by which they are befouled, and beloved youth thereby led astray. The same is inane, erroneous, empty chatter; and far removed from the foundation of Truth. Even at the present day it is blasphemously defended, tooth and nail, with all sorts of opinions, ideas, imaginations, and erroneous thoughts of the old heathen (who were held to be Sages), which were accepted as the Truth. . .
>
> This Philosophy, although, from my youth up, it was earnestly and diligently inculcated, and forced upon me, in the Schools (as unfortunately occurs to others at the present day), yet, by special interposition of the Holy Spirit, it became so suspected by me that I never would, nor could, torture my head, mind, and soul with it, nor persuade my heart that the same was a sacred thing, nor cleave unto it as others did; but, according to my childish judgment, let the matter rest there until, about the year 1587 or 1588, another philosophy came into my hands. At the same time I had, in my own mind, firmly resolved not to remain the least among my fellow scholars, but in due time to graduate in advance of all.

This sounds very much like Bacon's famous letter to his uncle Lord Burghley, in which he says "I have taken all knowledge for my province." Figulus continues:

> But it has pleased God otherwise in His Divine Providence, and all sorts of impediments on the part of my superiors hindered the course of my studies, until at last, in 1587-88, the books and writings of Theophrastus, of Roger Bacon, and of M. Isaac the Hollander, fell into my hands; in which I, especially in medicine (for they wrote about the Universal Stone and Medicine), saw and found a better foundation, and yet understood it not at first. But I took such a liking to the subject that I resolved not to die, nor yet to take my ease, until I had obtained this Universal Stone and Blessed Heavenly Medicine. However, the poverty of my parents and the impossibility of obtaining the necessary funds (for at that time but few princes and nobles patronized this study) compelled me unwillingly to relinquish my plan, although I was so eager for it that, for many months, I could not sleep on account of it. At last, in 1590, I found myself plunged by the devil and his friends into great misery, misfortune, and sickness, out

of which God mercifully helped me when my death would have been preferred to my recovery, and when, from reasons of poverty, I had been held to commerce against my will, by my relatives, suffering all manner of persecution, partly from the Anti-Christian mob, partly from false brethren, wife and friends, tortured, plagued and agitated, and thus thoroughly tried by the devil.

But having been rescued from the same by God's fatherly care, I turned my attention for some years to poetry, whereunto, when I found that it was irksome to all, I said good bye…

Appendix: *The Labyrinth of the World and the Paradise of the Heart* (1631)

Chapter 11: The Pilgrim Came among the Philosophers

Then my interpreter addressed me: "Now I shall lead you among the philosophers, whose task it is to discover the means of correcting all human deficiencies and to show the essence of true wisdom." "God grant that I shall at last learn something certain," said I. "Of course you will," he replied; "for these are men who know the truth of everything, without whose knowledge neither heaven manifests itself nor does the abyss hide anything; they guide human life nobly to virtue, enlighten communities and countries, and have God for their friend; for their wisdom penetrates His secrets." "Let us hurry, please," I urged; "let us go among them as quickly as possible." But when he brought me among these men, and I saw a crowd of these oldsters with their strange antics, I stood as if petrified. For there Bion sat still, Anacharsis strolled about, Thales flew, Hesiod plowed, Plato chased ideas in the air, Homer sand, Aristotle disputed, Pythagoras kept still, Epimenides slept, Archimedes tried to push the earth away, Solon was composing laws and Galen prescriptions, Euclid was measuring the hall, Cleobulus was peering into the future, Periander was defining duties, Pittacus was waging war, Bias was begging, Epictetus was serving, Seneca, sitting among tons of gold, was extolling poverty, Socrates was confiding to everybody that he knew nothing, Xenophon, on the contrary, was promising to teach everything to everybody, Diogenes, peering out of his barrel, was deriding all passersby, Timon was cursing all, Democritus was laughing at it all, Heraclitus, on the contrary, was weeping, Zeno was fasting, Epicurus was feasting, while Anaxarchus was holding forth that all these things were only apparent, not real. Moreover, there was a flock of smaller philosophical fry, each of whom was doing something extraordinary; but I neither remember nor care to recount it all. Observing it all, I said: "Are these, then, the wise men, the light of the world? Alas! Alas! I had hoped for better things! For these act like peasants in a tavern: they all howl, and each to a different tune." "You are a dunce," my interpreter retorted, "you do not understand such mysteries." Hearing that there were mysteries, I began to scrutinize the crowd meticulously, while my interpreter began to explain them to me. Straightway a man (called Paul of Tarsus) in a philosopher's garb, approached me and whispered into my ear: "If any man among you thinks he is wise in this world, let him become a fool that he may be wise. For the wisdom of the world is but foolishness with God. For it is written: The Lord knows the thoughts of the wise that they are futile." Perceiving that what my eyes have seen and my ears have heard agreed with this speech, I willingly acquiesced and said: "Let us go elsewhere." My interpreter scolded me for being such a fool, saying that when I might learn something among the wise, I ran away from them. But I pressed on in silence.

He came among the grammarians

We then entered a lecture room full of young and old, who, with pointers in their hands, were engaged in drawing letters, dashes, and dots; whenever any of them wrote or pronounced his formula differently from the rest, they either ridiculed or scolded him. Moreover, they hung some words on the wall and disputed as to what belonged to which; then they composed, separated, or transposed them variously. I looked at this for a while, but seeing nothing in it, I said: "These are but childish trivialities. Let us go elsewhere."

Among the rhetoricians

Thereupon we entered another hall where many were gathered with brushes in their hands, discussing how words, either written or escaping from the mouth into the air, could be painted green, red, black, white, or any other color desired. I inquired what the purpose of this procedure. "This is done in order that the hearer's brain may be colored in different ways," my interpreter replied. "Are these disguises intended to bring out truth or falsehood?" I continued. "Either one," he answered. "Then there is as much fraud and falsehood as truth and benefit in it," I remarked, and went out.

Among the poets

We then entered another place; and behold! a crowd of spry-looking adolescents weighing syllables in scales and arranging them in feet, meanwhile rejoicing over their work and skipping about. I was amazed and inquired what it all meant. "Of all literary arts," my interpreter explained, "this one is the most skillful and gay." "But what is it?" I inquired. "Whatever cannot be managed by simple coloring of the words," he answered, "is accomplished by this folding process." Noticing that those who were learning this art of word-folding consulted certain books, I also glanced into them and read their titles: *De Culice, De Passere, De Lesbia, De Priapo, De arte amandi, Metamorphoses, Encomia, Satirae*, or in a word, farces, poems, comedies, and all kinds of other frivolities. This made me somehow loathe the whole thing. Especially when I perceived that whenever anyone flattered those syllable-mongers, they expended all their art on his adulation; but whenever anyone displeased them, they showered him with sarcasms. Thus the art was used for nothing but flattery or defamation. Discerning what passionate folk they were, I gladly hurried away from them.

Among the dialecticians

Entering another building, we found that lenses for glasses were ground and sold there. I inquired what they were. *Notiones secundae*, they told me. Whoever possessed them could see not only the exterior of things, but to their very core; especially could one look into another's brain and scrutinize his mind. Many people came to buy these glasses, and the masters taught them how to put them on and, if need be, to readjust them. There were special master glass-grinders who had their workshops in obscure nooks; but they did not make the glasses identical. One made them large, another small; one round, another polygonal. Each praised his own wares and tried to attract buyers, while among themselves they quarreled perpetually and heckled each other. Some buyers purchased glasses from each of the makers, and put them all on; others selected and used only one pair. Thereupon some complained that even so they could not penetrate as deeply as they had been told, while others claimed that they could, and pointed to each other beyond the mind and all reason. But I noticed that not a few of these latter, venturing to step out, stumbled over boulders and stumps and fell into ditches, of which, as I had remarked before, the place was full. "How does it happen," I asked, "that although everything may be seen through the glasses, these people do not avoid the obstacles?" I was told that it was not the fault of the glasses, but of the people who did not know who to use them. The masters added, moreover, that it was not sufficient to possess the glasses of dialectic, but that the eyes must be cleared with the bright eye-salve of physics and mathematics. Therefore, they advised the buyers to repair to the other halls and to have their eyesight improved. Accordingly, they went, one here, another there. Thereupon, I said to my guides: "Let us follow as well." We did not go, however, until at the prompting of Mr. Searchall I had procured and put on several pairs of these glasses. It is true that I seemed able to discern somewhat more than before, and that a particular thing could be seen from several points of view. But still I insisted that we proceed to the place where I could try the eye-salve of which they had spoken.

Among the natural scientists

So we went, and they led me to a certain square in the center of which I saw a large, wide-spreading tree bearing diversely-shaped leaves and various fruit (all in hard shells); they called it Nature. A large number of philosophers had gathered around, examining it and explaining to each other what the name of each branch, leaf, or fruit was. "These, I hear, are learning the names of these things," I said, "but I do not perceive that they apprehend their real being." "Not everyone is able to do that," my interpreter answered; "nevertheless, watch these men here." I saw some of them break off the branches and open the leaves and the shell, and finding the nut, cracking it with such a force that they well-nigh broke their teeth: but they claimed to have broken the shells; then picking over the crushed mass, they boasted to have discovered the kernel, and surreptitiously showed it to a select few among the company. But when I diligently scrutinized the procedure, I perceived plainly that although they had indeed broken the outer husk and the integuement, the inner hard shell, containing the kernel, remained whole. Being thus aware of their immodest boasts and futile toil (for some of them had lost their sight and broken their teeth) I suggested that we go elsewhere.

Among the metaphysicians

Thereupon we entered another hall; and lo! it was full of philosophical gentlemen who were examining cows, asses, wolves, serpents, and various other beasts, birds, reptiles, as well as wood, stone, water, fire, clouds, stars, planets, and indeed even the angels; thereupon they held disputations among themselves as to how each creature could be deprived of its distinctive characteristics so that all might become alike. They first divested them of their form, then of their substance, and finally of all their "accidents", until nothing but the "being" remained. Then they quarreled whether all these things were one and the same; or whether they were all good; or whether they really were what they appeared to be, and about many other similar questions. Some of those observing them expressed their amazement at the surpassing keenness of the human wit that was able to fathom the essence of all things and to divest all corporeal beings of their corporeality; indeed, I myself began to be fascinated by these subtleties. Just then, however, a man stepped out, crying that all these studies were but fantasies, and exhorted all to abandon them. Thereupon some were indeed drawn after him; but others rose up and condemned them as heretics, accusing them of wishing to deprive philosophy of its highest art and, as it were, of decapitating knowledge. Having listened sufficiently to these wranglings, I went away.

Chapter 12: The Pilgrim Examines Alchemy

Thereupon Mr. Ubiquitous remarked: "Now come along, for I shall take you to a place where you will find the highest peak of human ingenuity, and show you an occupation so delightful that anyone who has once turned to it is never again willing to abandon it as long as he lives, because of the charm and delight which it affords his mind." I begged him not to delay in showing me. Thereupon he led me down into some cellars where I saw several rows of fireplaces, small ovens, kettles, and glass instruments, all shining brightly. Men tending the fires were gathering and piling on brushwood and blowing into it, or again extinguishing it, filling and pouring something from one glass into another. "Who are these folk, and what are they doing?" I asked. "They are the most ingenious of philosophers," my interpreter answered, "effecting instantly what the celestial sun with its heat can effect in the bowels of the earth only after a considerable number of years: they transform various metals into their highest category, namely, gold." "But for what purpose," I asked, "since iron and other metals are of more frequent use than gold?" "What a dunce you are!" he exclaimed, "don't you know that gold is the most precious of metals, and that he who has gold need fear no poverty?"

Lapis philosophicus

"Besides, that which has the potency to change metals into gold possesses other most astounding properties: for instance, it can preserve human health to the end of life, and ward off death for two or three hundred years. In fact, if men knew how to use it, they could make themselves immortal. For this stone is nothing less than the seed of life, the kernel and the quintessence of the universe, from which all animals, plants, metals, and the very elements derive their being." I was affrighted, hearing such astounding news, and asked: "Are these people, then, immortal?" "Not all are so fortunate as to discover the stone," he answered, "and those who find it do not always know how to use it effectively." "If I had the stone," I remarked, "I would take care to use it in such a way as to keep death away, and would procure plenty of gold for myself and others. But where is the stone to be found?" "It is prepared here," he answered. "In these small kettles?" I exclaimed. "Yes."

The mishaps of the alchemists

Full of curiosity, I walked about scrutinizing everything to learn what and how the thing was done; but I observed that not all fared equally. The fire of one was not hot enough: his mixture did not reach the boiling point. Another had too intense a fire, and his glass retorts cracked and something puffed out. As he explained it, the nitrogen had escaped; and he wept. Another, while pouring the liquid, spilled it or mixed it wrongly. Another burned his eyes out, and was thus unable to supervise the calcination and the fixation: or bleared his sight with smoke to such an extent that before he cleared his eyes the nitrogen escaped. Some died of asphyxiation from the smoke. But for the greatest part they did not have enough coal in their bags and were obliged to run about to borrow it elsewhere, while in the meantime their concoction cooled off and was utterly ruined. This was of very frequent, in fact of almost constant, occurrence. Although they did not tolerate anyone among themselves save such as possessed full bags, yet these seemed to have a way of drying up very rapidly, and soon grew empty: they were obliged either to suspend their operations or to run away to borrow.

After watching them, I said: "I see a good many here toil vain; but perceive none who succeeds in getting the stone. I also see that these people boil and burn both their gold and their lives, and often squander and burn both; but where are those with the heaps of gold and immortality?" "Naturally, they do not reveal themselves to you," my interpreter answered, "nor would I advise them so to do. Such a priceless thing must be kept secret. For if one of the rulers learned of such a man, he would immediately demand his surrender and the poor fellow would become no better than a prisoner for life; consequently, they must keep themselves in hiding."

Then I observed some of the scorched ones gather together, and turning my ear toward them, I heard them discuss the causes of their failures. One blamed the philosophers for their too involved description of the art; another lamented the brittleness of the glass implements; a third complained of an untimely and inauspicious aspect of the planets; a fourth was disgruntled with the earthly impurities of the mercury; a fifth complained of lack of capital. In short, there were so many causes of failure that I saw that they were at a loss to know how to mend their art. Thus when they left one after another, I left also.

Chapter 13: The Pilgrim Observes the Rosicrucians

Fama fraternitatis, anno 1612 latine ac germanice edita

Then I heard in the square the blare of a trumpet, and turning back I perceived a rider on horseback, calling the philosophers together. When a crowd of them gathered about him from all sides, he began to harangue them in five languages about the imperfections of the liberal arts and of philosophy generally. He announced that certain famous men, impelled by God, had ascertained and corrected all such imperfections, and restored the wisdom of mankind to the same degree of perfection which it had had in paradise before the Fall. To make gold, he said, is the least among hundreds of their accomplishments: for all nature stands naked and uncovered before them and they are able to transfer at pleasure the form of any creature to another. They know the languages of all nations, and are aware of all that is taking place everywhere in the world, including the New World, and are able to discourse among themselves even though they be thousands of miles apart. They also possess the stone, with which they are able to heal perfectly all kinds of diseases, and to impart long life. Thus, for example, their president, Hugo Alverda, had attained the age of five hundred and sixty-two years, and his colleagues not much less. And although they have kept themselves hidden for so many hundreds of years, during which time seven of them devoted themselves to the improvement of philosophy, they have now, at last, brought it all to perfection. Moreover, knowing that the reformation of the whole world is about to begin, they wish no longer to keep themselves in hiding, but announce quickly their willingness to share their priceless secrets with anyone whom they should recognize as being worthy. If any such makes himself known to them, be he of whatever language or nationality, they will learn of it, and no one will be left without a kindly answer. However, if any unworthy person should apply from motives of avarice or idle curiosity, such a person will not be able to learn anything about them.

Varia de fama judicia

Having finished his speech, the herald disappeared; looking about me at the learned, I saw them well-nigh terrified by the news. Gradually they began to put their heads together and to express their judgement about the matter, some in whispers, others aloud. Joining a group here and there, I listened: some were exceedingly glad, hardly knowing how to contain themselves for joy. They pitied their ancestors whose age had afforded them nothing comparable, and considered themselves blessed to be so freely offered a perfect philosophy: to know everything infallibly, to possess everything in abundance, and to live several hundred years without sickness or grey hairs — all to be had by anyone desiring it! They kept on repeating: "Happy, thrice happy, is our age!" Hearing these words, I myself began to rejoice, indulging in the hope of sharing, God willing, the blessings upon which the others were counting. But I saw others buried in deep thought, greatly perplexed what to think of the news. They wished it were true, but the matter appeared to them dubious and surpassing human reason. Others openly rejected it, declaring it to be a fraud and a deceit. "If these men have lived for so many centuries," they said, "why have they not revealed themselves sooner? If they are so sure of their cause, why do they not step out freely into the light, instead of squeaking like bats out of some obscure nook? Philosophy is well enough established and needs no reformation; should we allow it to be snatched out of our hands, we shall be left without any." Others even heaped terrible scoffing and abuse upon them, denouncing them as diviners, sorcerers, and demons incarnate.

Fraternitatem ambientes

In short, the whole square was filled with clamor, and almost all burned with the desire to reach the fraternity. Therefore, not a few of them wrote their supplications, some secretly, others openly, and sent them off, full of joy in anticipation of being received into the fraternity. But I perceived that after the supplications had gone to every conceivable nook, all were returned unanswered. Then their joyful hope was turned into grief: besides, they had to endure jeers of the sceptics. Some wrote another petition, and then a second, a third or even more, begging and imploring, in the name of all the Muses and in the most affecting manner, that the fraternity decline not a mind a thirst for knowledge. Some, impatient of delay, personally undertook the journey from one end of the world to the other, but lamented their misfortune in not being able to find those happy folk. Some ascribed the reason for their failure to their own unworthiness, others to the ill-will of the fraternity. Consequently, some fell into despair, while others tortured themselves by persisting in their endeavor to discover ever new ways of ascertaining the group's whereabouts, until I myself grew weary of waiting for the final outcome.

Continuatio

Then a trumpet blared again: when many ran out to find out what the sound imported, I joined them also. I saw a man setting up a booth, inviting the bystanders to examine and to buy his most wonderful mysteries; he claimed to have taken them from the treasures of the new philosophy, and assured all desirous of the secret wisdom would find satisfaction therein. Then many rejoiced that the holy Brotherhood of the Rose had openly and liberally shared its treasures and approaching, bought the wares. All articles put up for sale were enclosed in painted boxes, bearing attractive inscriptions such as: *Good Guide to the Large and the Small Cosmos*; *A Harmony of the Two Worlds*; *The Christian Cabala*; *The Case of Nature*; *The Castle of Primordial Matter*, *The Divin Magic*; *The General Tri-Trinity*; *The Triumphal Pyramid*; *Hallelujah*; and so forth. But the buyers were forbidden to open the boxes. For the efficacy of the secret wisdom was said to be so powerful that it operated by penetration, and would evaporate if the box were opened. Nevertheless, some of the more inquisitive could not refrain from opening their boxes and found them entirely empty! Thereupon, they showed them to others, who also opened their boxes and likewise found nothing. Then they raised a cry of "Fraud! Fraud!" and assaulted the dealer with fury. He attempted to pacify them by saying that the most secret part of the mystery consisted in the fact that these things were invisible to all save the sons of science; and since barely one out of a thousand possessed the proper qualifications, he, the dealer, was not to blame for it.

Eventus famae

The buyers for the greatest part were pacified thereby; in the meantime the dealer packed up his wares, while the spectators dispersed in very different humors, one here, another there. But whether or not anyone had discovered the new mysteries, I have hitherto been unable to learn. This only I know; that thereafter everything quieted down and those who had been formerly running and rushing about the most, were found sitting in obscure corners with their mouths shut. Either they had been (as some thought) admitted to the mysteries upon an oath that they keep them secret; or (as it appeared to me observing them from under my glasses) were ashamed of their blasted hopes and misspent effort. Thus everything passed and quieted down as clouds disperse after a rainless storm. I said to my companions: "Are all these things, then, an utter failure? Oh, my disappointed hopes! Hearing such boastful promises, I expected to find a profitable pasture for my mind." My interpreter answered: "Who knows but it might yet materialize? Perhaps they know their hour when and to whom to reveal themselves." "Should I wait for such an event, when I have not seen a single instance of success among so many thousands of men more learned than I am? I do not care to gape any longer: let us go away," I said.